Physical
Wireha
(from the Ame

Back: Strong and firm.

Tail: Extends from the back in a continuation of the topline. It is docked by one-third to one-half length.

Hindquarters: The thighs are long and well muscled. Angulation in balance with the front. The legs are vertical with the hocks turning neither in nor out. The stifle and hock joints are strong and well angulated.

Coat: One of the distinguishing features of the breed. It is a double coat. The outer coat is medium length, straight and wiry, never curly or woolly. The obligatory undercoat consists of a fine, thick down, which provides insulation as well as water resistance.

Size: 22 to 24 inches for males, 20 to 22 inches for females.

Wirehaired Pointing Griffon

By Nikki Moustaki

8 History of the Wirehaired Pointing Griffon

Though the French lay claim to this "supreme gundog," the Wirehaired Pointing Griffon was a gift to the hunting world from the son of a wealthy Dutch banker. Follow the trail of the original Griffs of continental Europe in the 19th century to the hunting fields of America today. A history of breed clubs and a detailed timeline will further your knowledge of the development of this wonderful gundog.

20 Characteristics of the Wirehaired Pointing Griffon

Learn why the Griff is known as the "best-kept secret of the Sporting Group" through discussions on his physical traits, temperament, personality and trainability. Is your home suitable for this goofy, energetic and faithful gundog and are you an appropriate owner? Also discussed are health concerns in the breed.

30 Breed Standard for the Wirehaired Pointing Griffon

Learn the requirements of a well-bred Wirehaired Pointing Griffon by studying the description of the breed set forth in the American Kennel Club standard and the French working standard. Show dogs, hunting dogs and pets must possess key characteristics as outlined in the breed standard.

36 Your Puppy Wirehaired Pointing Griffon

Find out about how to locate a well-bred Wirehaired Pointing Griffon puppy. Discover which questions to ask the breeder and what to expect when visiting the litter. Prepare for your puppy-accessory shopping spree. Also discussed are home safety, the first trip to the vet, socialization and solving basic puppy problems.

64 Proper Care of Your Wirehaired Pointing Griffon

Cover the specifics of taking care of your Wirehaired Pointing Griffon every day: feeding for the puppy, adult and senior dog; coat care and other routine grooming; and exercise needs for your dog. Also discussed are ID, boarding and traveling safely with your pet.

82 Training Your Wirehaired Pointing Griffon

Begin with the basics of training the puppy and adult dog. Learn the principles of house-training the Wirehaired Pointing Griffon, including the use of crates and basic scent instincts. Get started by introducing the pup to his collar and leash and progress to the basic commands. Find out about obedience classes and training for other activities.

Contents

Healthcare of Your Wirehaired Pointing Griffon 107

By Lowell Ackerman DVM, DACVD
Become your dog's healthcare advocate and a well-educated canine keeper. Select a skilled and able veterinarian. Discuss pet insurance, vaccinations and infectious diseases, the neuter/spay decision and a sensible, effective plan for parasite control, including fleas, ticks and worms.

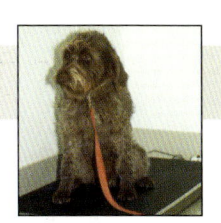

Showing Your Wirehaired Pointing Griffon 132

Step into the center ring and find out about the world of showing pure-bred dogs. Acquaint yourself with the basics of AKC conformation showing and find out about other types of competition for the Wirehaired Pointing Griffon: obedience and field trials, agility competition and tracking and hunting tests.

Behavior of Your Wirehaired Pointing Griffon 148

Analyze the canine mind to understand what makes your Wirehaired Pointing Griffon tick. Learn how to recognize and handle potential canine behavior problems: different types of aggression, separation anxiety and chewing.

Index 156

KENNEL CLUB BOOKS®
WIREHAIRED POINTING GRIFFON
ISBN: 1-59378-364-7

Copyright © 2006, 2007 • Kennel Club Books® • A Division of BowTie, Inc.
40 Broad Street, Freehold, NJ 07728 USA
Cover Design Patented: US 6,435,585 B2 • Printed in South Korea

Library of Congress Cataloging-in-Publication Data

Moustaki, Nikki, 1970-
  Wirehaired pointing griffon / by Nikki Moustaki.
    p. cm.
  ISBN 1-59378-364-7
  1. Wirehaired pointing griffon. I. Title.
  SF429.W57M68 2006
  636.752--dc22
                    2006011590

10 9 8 7 6 5 4 3 2

Photography by Philippe Roca
with additional photos by:

Paulette Braun, Callea, Alan and Sandy Carey, Carolina Biological Supply, Isabelle Français, Carol Ann Johnson, Bill Jonas, Dr. Dennis Kunkel, Tam C. Nguyen, Phototake, Jean Claude Revy, Chuck Tatham and Alice van Kempen.

Illustrations by Patricia Peters.

All rights reserved. No part of this book may be reproduced in any form, by photostat, scanner, microfilm, xerography or any other means, or incorporated into any information retrieval system, electronic or mechanical, without the written permission of the copyright owner.

HISTORY OF THE
WIREHAIRED POINTING GRIFFON

The word "griffon," as a generic term, refers to a shaggy, rough-coated dog with a downy undercoat. Dogs of the griffon type have been known in Europe since the mid-1500s, hundreds of years before the advent of the versatile gundog that is the subject of this book. A French word, "griffon" appears in the names of a few American Kennel Club breeds, such as the Brussels Griffon, Petit Basset Griffon Vendéen and, of course, the Wirehaired Pointing Griffon. The Wirehaired Pointing Griffon (WPG) for generations has inspired an unrivaled passion and devotion from its followers. A superb gundog, a loyal house dog and a gentle friend to the children of the family, the WPG is still little known to the dog layperson but has long been a versatile treasure to hunters all over the globe.

Though the French lay claim to developing the "Griff," the

Few dogs can compare to the WPG in terms of hunting skills, devotion to his owners and a gentle demeanor with all family members, including the children.

breed was actually started by a young Dutchman named Eduard K. Korthals (1851–1896). As the son of a wealthy banker and shipbuilder, Korthals had the time on his hands to develop a dog that suited his favorite pastime—hunting. His father bred cattle, so Korthals already understood something of selective breeding and genetics and sought to create an all-terrain, close-working, pointing and retrieving gundog that would be easy to care for and train. He was partial to the griffon, which occurred in many forms throughout Europe, and set out to find the perfect "type" (size, coat, temperament, etc.) in order to develop the ideal dog patterned in his mind. Since Korthals denied using anything other than griffons in his breeding lines, it's difficult to ascertain which breeds or types of dog he incorporated into this new breed. Undoubtedly he used various spaniels and setters that were available to him in Holland and possibly the Barbet and Otterhound. Korthals actually did cross with a German Shorthaired Pointer but the results were disastrous, so he didn't pursue it.

The Wirehaired Pointing Griffon, or the "Korthals Griffon," as the WPG came to be known, began in earnest in 1874 when Korthals started his breeding program with a bitch named Mouche, a brown-and-gray griffon who was reported to be a good

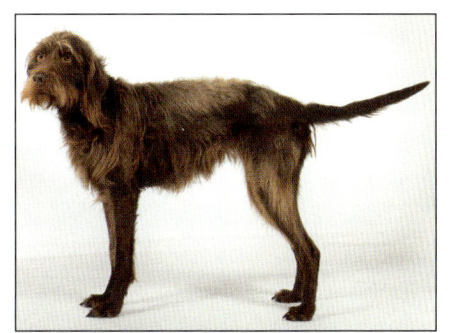

The Pudelpointer originated in Germany, where it was created in the late 1800s by Baron von Zedlitz by combining outstanding Pointers and Poodle-type dogs.

Two German Wirehaired Pointers, distinguishable by their eyebrows, mustaches and beards.

The German Longhaired Pointer is distinguishable by its wavy long coat and large size, standing up to 27.5 inches at the shoulder.

The Griffon Bleu de Gascogne, one of the many wirehaired hunting dogs of France, may well be in the make-up of the Wirehaired Pointing Griffon.

WIREHAIRED POINTING GRIFFON

CANIS LUPUS
"Grandma, what big teeth you have!" The gray wolf, a familiar figure in fairy tales and legends, has had its reputation tarnished and its population pummeled over the centuries. Yet it is the descendants of this much-feared creature to which we open our homes and hearts. Our beloved dog, *Canis domesticus*, derives directly from the gray wolf, a highly social canine that lives in elaborately structured packs. In the wild, the gray wolf can range from 60 to 175 pounds, standing between 25 and 40 inches in height.

hunter in a variety of landscapes. The other original dogs, or "Korthals Patriarchs," were Janus, Satan, Banco, Hector and Junon. The bitch Trouvee, a result of a breeding between Mouche and Janus, resulted in the type of coat that Korthals was looking for, and a mating between Trouvee and Banco produced Moustache I, Lina and Querida. The lineage of all true WPGs can be traced to these dogs.

Korthals, who was then working as an advance agent for the French Duke of Penthièvre, attended many field events, praising the merits of his dogs and informing the hunting community of Europe about the concept of his ideal hunting dog. In 1877 Korthals was offered the use of a large kennel in Germany, owned by Prince Albrecht of Solms-Braunfels. He moved his dogs to Germany and dedicated the next 20 years to the development of his Korthals Griffon. During this time, he worked with over 600 dogs, keeping only 60 that he considered correct for his new breed. He did extensive line-breeding (mating dogs of the same family to a common ancestor); thus in some pedigrees one foundation dog will occur many times, sometimes in dozens of places.

The breed became successful very early on, with Korthals competing the dogs in field trials and conformation shows. Though a fatal disease struck his kennel in 1882, killing 16 dogs, Korthals and his gundog friends all over Europe, particularly in France, were not daunted and continued developing the breed. Korthals died at 44 years of age on July 4, 1896, of laryngeal cancer.

A Griff stands proudly in the field with a fellow talented gundog of Continental origin, the Spinone Italiano.

Before Korthals' untimely death, a split occurred among advocates of the breed. The Germans wanted a certain type of dog, and the French wanted another—both from the WPG. Once Korthals was gone, the rift opened even further. World War I, beginning in 1914, significantly hindered the breed's progress in Germany, while French breeding took off and created what is essentially today a French dog with pan-European origins. Today the WPG exists mainly in France with about 14,000 dogs, while in Germany there are probably fewer than 600 breed members, about the same number in Italy and 200 to 300 dogs in each Holland and Belgium.

It is not known whether the French fell in love with the breed for its adept hunting ability or its personality. German hunting dogs, like the German Shorthaired Pointer, are like machines in the field, working consistently and tirelessly. The WPG is more of an artist, sensitive and a little moody, though he can also be consistent and driven. He can take a field trial by storm or not perform at all, depending on how he is feeling that day. The French say that the Griff will "invent" birds in the field—they go places where the other dogs haven't thought to look. The WPG is also a much softer dog and far more laid-back. According to Philippe Roca, vice president of the American Wirehaired Pointing Griffon Association, a trainer should be as laid-back as the dog. "When you train, you need to be very creative and make training fun for the dog. Appeal to your dog's intelligence. Channel his drive. You can't tell him what to do. You use the Griff's instinctual drive and channel it where you want. You can't train the dog like you train a robot."

The French school of training for the breed is also different. For the French, the WPG is a bird dog only. The Germans use the dog to hunt fur-bearing animals and to do blood-tracking as well, often with the handlers on horseback, which the French do not do. The two countries are still split on this issue.

The first WPG registered with the American Kennel Club (AKC) in 1887 was Zoletta, a bitch who came to the United States and was recorded under the breed "Russian Setter (Griffon)." At that time, breeds with copious facial hair were supposed to have originated in the Siberian area, and so were registered incorrectly. In 1916, an official breed standard was established in the United States, and the Westminster Kennel Club Dog Show boasted 16 competing WPGs. By 1929, the WPG was registered in the American Field Dog Stud Book and competed in hunting and pointing events. Unfortunately, the two world wars put a damper on the propagation of the WPG, and serious breeding ceased.

The WPG found its way back to the United States again after World War II, when a group of

A strong and skilled worker, the Griff is not all business—the breed's charm and personality are evident in this lounging pack.

servicemen brought back the dogs they had seen and admired in France, Germany and Holland. The breed thrived, gaining loyal devotees in the many years following.

THE WPG FELLOWSHIP

The first WPG club was started by E. K. Korthals and his friends on July 29, 1888, and it was called the International Wirehaired Pointing Griffon Club. Specialty clubs in individual countries followed: the Royal Belgium Griffon Club began in 1895; the Club Français du Griffon d'Arrêt a Poil Dur Korthals commenced in 1901 in France; De Nederlandse Griffonclub initiated in 1911 in Holland; and the Griffon Club of America began in 1916, the year in which the official breed standard was instituted.

The Griffon Club of America fell apart under the pressure of World War II. But after the war, when the newly imported Griffs appeared in the States, Lt. Colonel Thomas Rogers and other breed devotees formed the Wirehaired Pointing Griffon Club of America (WPGA) in 1951. The breed flourished for over 30 years, but a rift eventually overtook the breed again.

In the late 1970s and early '80s, a faction of the WPG fancy was discontented with the quality of Griffs in the US and expressed the desire for better hunting dogs.

The faction believed that there was too much random breeding that wasn't well managed or well considered. The club started a committee to identify good breeding and began to hunt-test the litters of specific dogs. Those particular pups did not show well. The committee became frustrated at what they perceived to be the lack of "good" Griffs in North America. Someone outside the club suggested outcrossing the breed to German Wirehaired Pointers. Another advisor, a member of the breeding committee, suggested that the Griff would be best crossed with another hunting gundog, the Cesky Fousek (pronounced CHESkee FOWseck), a Czech breed which is similar in appearance to the WPG but whose hunting manner and disposition are more comparable to those of the German Wirehaired Pointer.

Even when relaxing, the WPG is keen, alert and ready to go.

WIREHAIRED POINTING GRIFFON

The 2004 American Wirehaired Pointing Griffon Association specialty show was judged by Marian Mason Hodesson and won by Ch. Flatbrook Kyjo's What a Sport, JH. A total of 42 WPGs competed.

This breed nearly died off during World War II even though the Czech government had been trying to resurrect it. Arrangements were made and the first Fouseks were brought over to the States. The outcrossed dogs were successful in competition, much to the delight of the group that supported this decision.

However, another faction of the club refused to taint the bloodlines that Korthals had so carefully created. This steadfast group did not approve of the crossbreeding and held that these new dogs (often called Foufons by this group) were not true WPGs, though the WPG/Fousek group held that they were.

The split was definite. The pure-bred faction went off on its own to create the American Wirehaired Pointing Griffon Association (AWPGA). In 1991 the AWPGA was recognized by the AKC as the official parent club for the breed. The Wirehaired Pointing Griffon Club of America is currently not recognized by the American Kennel Club (AKC), United Kennel Club (UKC), Canadian Kennel Club (CKC), Fédération Cynologique

Internationale (FCI), North American Versatile Hunting Dog Association (NAVHDA), American Field or the European Griffon and Fousek organizations. These organizations do not register or test the WPG/Fousek cross. Because of this, the Wirehaired Pointing Griffon Club of America created its own registry, wrote its own standard and began holding its own field trial competitions.

Comparatively speaking, the WPG/Fousek cross is a more "square" dog, whereas the Griffon is more "rectangular," longer than it is tall. Some of the dogs are also bigger. The mechanics of the dog has also changed. Its coat is a little tougher, as is its mentality, which is more like that of a German Wirehaired Pointer. These are not "bad" dogs—they are suited for the hunt and do well in field trials, but they are not pure-bred WPGs. The two groups are still philosophically divided, and heated discussions still occur. Nevertheless, members of both groups remain friendly, though neither will accept the other's perspective on the matter.

Today there's a healthy stock of WPGs in the United States. The WPG community is still very small, and most of the breeders know what the others are doing. When a litter is whelped, it's not unusual for most of the community to know about it.

Because the community is small, each breeder needs the others to keep the bloodlines strong and healthy. Dogs are still imported from Europe, primarily from France, and semen is also imported and used by breeders who want to improve their stock. Somewhere in the range of 400 to 500 Griff puppies are produced in

Best of Breed at Westminster in 2000, Ch. Jerome von Herrenhausen was shown by Cheryl Cates under judge Dr. Bernard E. McGivern, Jr.

the United States each year.

Perhaps the most important goal of the 21st century for the American Wirehaired Pointing Griffon Association is to prevent another split, this time between those who show their dogs in conformation events and those who hunt. The AWPGA would like conformation dogs to also achieve top field results. As it stands, it's often the case that the WPGs appearing at the weekend dog shows will be hunting in the field the following weekend, no matter what trophy or ribbon they bring home. The WPG, above everything, is a sporting/hunting breed which was bred for field work. The AWPGA's emphasis is to continue breeding dogs that meet the breed standard and that can still hunt with the best of 'em.

THE GRIFF ON THE HUNT
The Griff is indeed the consummate hunter, but it also competes successfully in agility events, obedience trials and tracking tests. Its proponents call it "the best-kept secret of the Sporting Group." The breed's versatility is what appeals to most of its fans. These dogs hunt successfully in all terrains and all weather, and they are competent swimmers. The breed was originally produced to hunt upland game birds, but it will also retrieve waterfowl and track and point on fur-bearing animals as well. It is known as an "all-game" dog.

Bill Marlow, president of the American Wirehaired Pointing Griffon Association, hunts his WPGs for pheasant and quail on the eastern shore of Maryland and hunts with the same dogs in canyons in Idaho on horseback. He has hunted ducks in Alaska and geese in Virginia with his dogs. "They swim and they have webbed feet and a dual coat like a Chesapeake Bay Retriever, and yet they'll point and retrieve upland game at the same time," said

The Griff thrives on doing his job and on his owner's praise.

Marlow. "You can go duck hunting early in the morning, and when the ducks stop flying you can get up out of the blind and walk out into the field and go quail hunting, and the dog will find and point quail and will hold that point and retrieve the quail for you."

The WPG has deep roots in the hunting dogs of Europe. As a result, the hunting instinct is very dominant in these dogs, without exception. Puppies will even begin pointing game at seven weeks old. Most people who own and breed these dogs will say, emphatically, that this dog is not a pet. This is not to say that the Griff isn't a great companion because he is indeed a sensitive family dog, able to read moods and sprawl happily at his owners' feet at the end of a day of rigorous hunting or running.

The Griff's hunting style is more "European," being a close-ranging hunter, bred to hunt with a human on foot, not on horseback. How far WPGs range depends on the type of cover and terrain, and they generally hunt in front of their human companion, though they will fall behind if the hunter passes a tightly sitting bird. Because they range close, voice commands and hand signals are ideal for WPGs.

Though they are known to be close-ranging hunters, some individuals have their own idea of how they should behave in the field. Bill Jensen, an AWPGA member and WPG breeder, once had a dog with an unusual hunting style. "I had one dog that was a 'run-off,'" said Jensen. "He was absolutely self-driven. He wasn't a team player. He was a French import and a wild, crazy dog—a very talented dog—but that one characteristic was frustrating. I never used him for breeding."

With a wiry coat to protect him in the field, the WPG is well suited to working in many types of terrain.

The versatile Griff can be an excellent retriever in water and on land if properly trained.

Breeders are adamant that the WPG does not end up in "pet-only" homes. Not only does that situation eliminate dogs from the preciously guarded breeding pool in the US, it also prevents the dogs from doing what they were created for—hunting. The dog comes alive when he's hunting. The moment the owner puts on his hunting vest, the dog knows that they are going out into the field.

There are a few Griffs each year that are destined for pet homes, usually those dogs that aren't "acceptable" in terms of temperament and conformation. These dogs will be spayed or neutered and sold at a lesser price. It's still important, however, that the dog be allowed to exercise himself by running as if on a hunt; according to WPG breeders and owners, jogging, walking or bicycling the dog around will not do. For the most part, even those dogs with minor conformational faults are still generally sold to hunting families and turn out to be remarkable hunters.

These are not city-dwelling dogs, though they are quite adaptable. They are more suited for country living where wide open spaces afford them the ability to dash around. The breed's interest in the outdoors will not fade just because its owners do not hunt or hunt only occasionally.

Many hunters compete in AKC hunt tests where the WPGs excel over such dogs as the English Setter, German Shorthaired Pointer and Pointer. The WPGs are often the envy of the owners of other breeds. Marlow remembers fondly the first hunt test he went to with a WPG. "On the second day of the test I came up to the line and some of the fellows who didn't know the dog with me said, 'The guy's got a Poodle! Look at that!' The other guy turned to the first guy and said, 'I saw this dog yesterday, and you're going to wish you had one of those Poodles!' Well, we started, and we didn't get 20 feet before my dog was pointing a bird. There weren't supposed to be any birds for another half mile, but she goes on point anyway, and I was really embarrassed. I pulled on her and said, 'Let's go,' but the judge said

WPG DEVELOPMENTAL TIMELINE

1851	Eduard Karel Korthals born—Amsterdam, The Netherlands
1867	Mouche whelped
1870–71	Franco-Prussian War
1873	Korthals begins serious breeding program
1874–77	Korthals acquires Mouche, Janus, Junon, Banco, Hector and Satan
1875	Banco whelped
1877–79	Korthals moves to Biebesheim am Rhein, Germany
1879	Donna acquired in Germany—longer coat
1882	Illness destroys 16 young dogs in Korthals's kennel
1885	Vesta leased as a brood bitch. Good producer—rough coat
1887	Korthals and 16 other breeders sign and publish the breed standard
1887	Zoletta registered with AKC
1888	International Griffon Club formed
1895	Southern German Griffon Club in Bavaria formed
1895	Royal Belgium Griffon Club formed
1896	Korthals dies
1901	Club Français du Griffon d'Arrêt a Poil Dur Korthals formed in France
1911	De Nederlandse Griffonclub formed in The Netherlands
1916	The Griffon Club of America (GCA) formed and breed standard adopted
1916	Sixteen Griffons exhibited at Westminster Kennel Club
1917	New *Country Life* magazine article published, peaking interest in the breed
1939–45	World War II—serious breeding activity stopped due to war—GCA ceases to exist
1951	New club formed—Wirehaired Pointing Griffon Club of America (WPGCA)
1980s	WPGCA splits into two groups; those wanting to crossbreed with Cesky Fousek and those who don't
1991	American Wirehaired Pointing Griffon Association formed by those choosing not to crossbreed (AWPGA)
1991	AKC recognizes AWPGA as official national parent club for Griffons in the US

Chart courtesy of the American Wirehaired Pointing Griffon Association

I'd better step into the bush, and sure enough a bird took off! We were probably the fifth or sixth brace, so that meant that there were no less than ten dogs that had run right past that quail and never stopped."

Overall, the WPG is an energetic hunter and a charming companion, often surprising in his abilities. For the avid hunter, this breed is a blessing, an exceptional instrument and a winning cohort, achieving successes worthy of ample bragging rights.

CHARACTERISTICS OF THE

WIREHAIRED POINTING GRIFFON

The handsome chestnut-marked dog with the huge expressive eyes, bushy eyebrows and beard and that charming, characteristic disheveled coat could only be one animal—the Wirehaired Pointing Griffon. But that furry face is deceiving; under the Benji-like tousled tresses is a determined hunter whose magnetism is outweighed only by his superb instincts, high energy level and keen desire to please.

PHYSICAL TRAITS
The Wirehaired Pointing Griffon is a medium-sized, double-coated hunting dog typically used for pointing and retrieving upland game but will track fur-bearing animals as well. The male weighs 55–70 pounds on average and is 22–24 inches at the shoulder; the female is generally 45–55 pounds and 20–22 inches at the shoulder. Only the French disqualify for height, meaning if the dogs don't

The strong hunting instinct and tousled look of the WPG is passed from generation to generation by responsible breeders.

fall within range, they are disqualified—50–55 cm for females (with a "tolerance" for a 56-cm bitch if she's exceptional) and 55–60 cm (with a tolerance of 61 cm for males). The dogs aren't measured in the show ring in the United States—if a dog falls half an inch or so above the height for the standard, the judge would have to have a keen eye to notice it. Some of the European WPGs, often the German-bred dogs, are much larger than their American (or French) counterparts, though this is considered a fault. The dog should be slightly longer than it is tall, giving it a "rectangular" shape; it should not be a "square" dog.

The WPG's outer coat is shaggy and coarse, and the undercoat is soft and insulating, a perfect combination for a hunting dog who works in heavy cover, marsh and water. The coat is resistant to burs and other prickly woodsy objects, though owners should go over the coat after each run in the field to make sure that it's clean and free of debris. The dog often looks "unkempt," which is exactly how this breed should look; even the best of conformation WPGs have a "shaggy" look.

According to the American Kennel Club standard, the coat should be "steel gray with brown markings, frequently chestnut brown, or roan, white and brown; white and orange also acceptable. A uniformly brown coat, all white coat, or white and oranges are less desirable. A black coat disqualifies." The coat takes two to three years to fully develop. In a show dog, the nose should always be brown but sometimes occurs in pink as a deviation.

The tail is docked to protect it during hunting. It's docked by one-third to one-half, still allowing the dog ample length to communicate with his tail. The breed's natural tail is thin and sparsely coated, and can be easily injured in the field or home if undocked. In Holland and Belgium, a Griff in the ring cannot have a docked tail; the French are scheduled to adopt this no-docking law in 2008. The reason

Ready for the hunt, the Griff is an all-weather, all-terrain, "do-it-all" companion in the field.

is humane. The French have already changed the standard for the tail by adding one sentence about its appearance. In many countries in Europe, it's forbidden to cut the tail of any dog.

The ears are natural (untrained and uncut) and flap over the ear openings to protect the ears from injury while the dog is on hunt through tall brush. The hair inside the ears must be plucked regularly to prevent infection. Dogs that swim are particularly susceptible to this problem.

How the Griff moves is of particular importance as well. The WPG is expected to cover ground tirelessly at medium speed and have perfect coordination between front and rear legs. According to the French working standard for the breed, "The general running style of the Griffon is that of a galloper, with a slight rocking movement from front to rear around the center of gravity. The feline pace, supple and skimming gallop is characteristic."

One distinguishing Griff characteristic is his bushy beard and the ability of the dog to soak up what seems like an entire bowlful of water into his beard and then slop it around the house and on every human leg he comes in contact with. Where there are thirsty Griffs, there are puddles of water.

TEMPERAMENT AND PERSONALITY

Goofy, funny, serious, aloof, driven, energetic, passionate, faithful—all of these words describe the Griff. As with any breed, personality and tempera-

> ### THE AGE OF ROBO-DOG
> Studies at the Center for the Human-Animal Bond show that children who interact with pets benefit physiologically, socially and educationally. Dogs, in particular, increase children's learning capacities and expand their abilities to function in social situations. Families with young children commonly add a canine to their homes.
>
> Enter Robo-dog. Efforts to create a robotic canine companion are fast underway, and there have been some interesting results. It is the hope of scientists that the interaction between children and robotic dogs will shed light on the physical, mental, moral and social concepts of such relationships. Robotic dogs offer some advantages over real dogs—they don't require food or water and never have accidents indoors. Even so, Robo-dogs will never take the place of real dogs—even George Jetson's futuristic family included Astro, a real-live dog! It is curious that 21st-century humans would invest so much money and energy into inventing robots to do for us what dogs have been doing for centuries for nothing more than a pat on the head and a bowl of food.

ment vary with the individual, but one thing is for certain—WPGs are people-oriented dogs, easy to live with and as comfortable in a home setting as they are in the field. Many people who are used to more "hyper" breeds are pleased with the Griff's ability to "settle" once inside the home. This isn't a bounce-off-the-wall breed, though a WPG that doesn't get enough exercise or attention can certainly do some damage to a home in an effort to entertain himself or burn off some excess energy.

On the hunt, the Griff is a "team player," keeping track of his human companion. It's a close working breed, much different from some of the other pointers. They tend to "check in" with their humans during a hunt and range according to the type of cover—farther in lower brush, closer in dense or taller brush. Some individuals can be "run-off" dogs, but that isn't the norm.

The WPG is known to be great with children and is generally happy to meet guests. Individuals can be bouncy when excited but if trained correctly will calm down easily. They make good sentries but aren't great guard dogs in general; they may be more interested to see if an intruder has a treat than protect the house from him. However, some individuals can be quite possessive and will not allow intruders to cross their boundaries, protecting what's theirs. They have a high tolerance for human activities, which makes them easy to keep. They will perform in the show ring on Monday, hunt on Tuesday and play ball all day with the kids on Wednesday.

Children should be taught to respect the Griff. The dog will tolerate a little tail-pulling and beard-grabbing from a small child, but he shouldn't have to. In general, the breed is known as a good family dog, gentle and protective, but he has his limits. Most breeders prefer to place their pups with families who have kids of six years of age or older. The kids in the family should never have the sole responsibility for the dog.

A close and lasting bond is the goal of proper, early socialization with children. There are many wonderful fishing days ahead for these best friends.

Most of these dogs are very friendly, but some individuals do remain aloof. Often, this is an attraction point for owners. Instead of having a waggy, exuberant dog knocking things over in the house, they prefer a more laid-back individual, which can be found in this breed.

Puppies learn very quickly and will point as early as seven weeks old, though some individuals don't learn the finer skills of hunting until they are older. Many owners profess that these dogs do not even need to be trained to hunt—they do it naturally. All dogs in the Sporting Group have basic hunting instincts. However, some methods of hunting need training, and the Griff is an eager student. Because of his intelligence, the Griff can be much harder to train at the highest level. If you push too hard, you break the dog, and if you don't push hard enough, the dog won't perform. You have to be a very apt, smart trainer to work with a WPG. This is not a dog for a novice.

Even though the WPG is a hunting dog, he doesn't do well with kennel life. He prefers to be a house dog, living in close contact with his family. A Griff left in a kennel will pine for his favorite humans and may develop some nasty behavior issues. This dog also definitely needs a fenced yard where he can run, but not run away—he loves his humans, but he loves to run and hunt too.

Introducing a WPG pup to other animals in the house should be done as early as possible. The Griff has a strong prey drive, and an older dog that has not been socialized to cats and other swift-moving animals might hunt them and even kill them if you're not there to intervene. Further, never trust a Griff around pet birds, hamsters and the like. Neighborhood cats and passing squirrels will definitely not be tolerated in the yard. While on the topic of animals to avoid, the Griff's prey drive is so powerful that he won't be deterred by a skunk or a porcupine, should he happen to run across one. You may find yourself having to "de-skunk" your dog or spend time pulling lots of quills out of his face.

TRAINABILITY

The WPG is a member of the American Kennel Club's Sporting Group and the United Kennel Club's Gundog Group. He loves to please his owner, as most sporting dogs do. He excels at obedience, agility, search and rescue and, of course, hunting. These dogs can learn to hunt just about any game, though they were bred to hunt upland fowl. Griffs will pursue boar and stag, will hunt with falcons and will track blood, as is common in Germany, and can even be trained to hunt bear. The

Proper training will yield a top-notch hunting dog who will stop at nothing to please his owner. The WPG is poetry in motion in the field.

keen senses of these dogs allow them to track, retrieve, hunt with humans on horseback and do just about anything else asked of them in the field. Some individuals can become gun-shy with poor training methods, though in no greater numbers than in any other breed. In other words, there's no real temperament problem in the WPG, and this gun-shyness can be solved using desensitization methods.

Training must be done with a light hand. Heavy-handed and rough training methods do not work with this dog and will only succeed in taxing the relationship between dog and owner. The Griff will hold a grudge and remember exactly the treatment afforded him. Someone who can't control his temper should think of getting another breed or no dog at all.

This breed is particularly intelligent and doesn't need an extreme training protocol. It does require, however, a lot of positive reinforcement and praise.

Many breed enthusiasts seem to prefer females to males, finding them more eager to learn, less stubborn and more physically agile than males. But there's no definitive way to choose a Griff puppy, male or female, that will be easily trainable or make a great hunter. Simply choose the sex of the puppy that you want and pick the one from the litter that most attracts you. You're as likely to get a good dog or a fair one whether you use this method or sit around for days watching the pups. There are temperament tests, however, that might separate the slackers from the go-getters, but whether or not a puppy performs well

DO YOU KNOW ABOUT HIP DYSPLASIA?

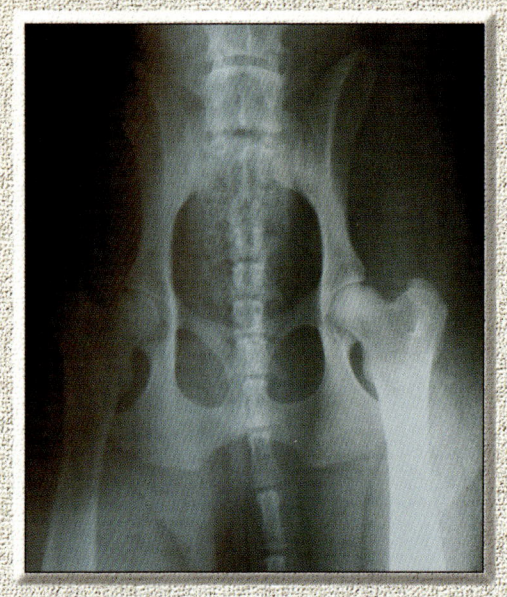

X-ray of a dog with "Good" hips.

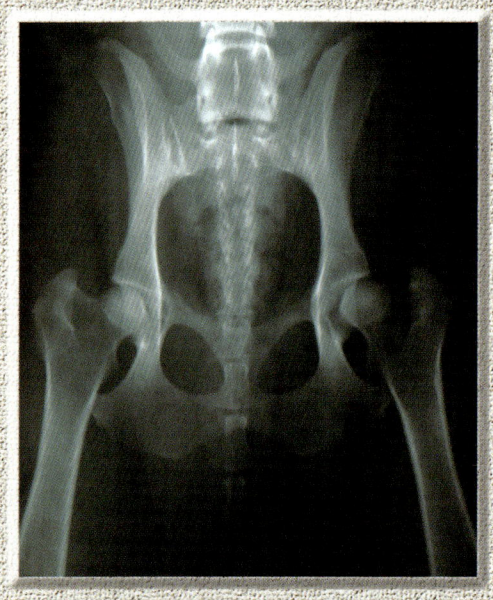

X-ray of a dog with "Moderate" dysplastic hips.

Hip dysplasia is a fairly common condition found in pure-bred dogs. When a dog has hip dysplasia, his hind leg has an incorrectly formed hip joint. By constant use of the hip joint, it becomes more and more loose, wears abnormally and may become arthritic.

Hip dysplasia can only be confirmed with an x-ray, but certain symptoms may indicate a problem. Your dog may have a hip dysplasia problem if he walks in a peculiar manner, hops instead of smoothly runs, uses his hind legs in unison (to keep the pressure off the weak joint), has trouble getting up from a prone position or always sits with both legs together on one side of his body.

As the dog matures, he may adapt well to life with a bad hip, but in a few years the arthritis develops and many dogs with hip dysplasia become crippled.

Hip dysplasia is considered an inherited disease and can be diagnosed definitively by x-ray only when the dog is two years old, although symptoms often appear earlier. Some experts claim that a special diet might help your puppy outgrow the bad hip, but the usual treatments are surgical. The removal of the pectineus muscle, the removal of the round part of the femur, reconstructing the pelvis and replacing the hip with an artificial one are all surgical interventions that are expensive, but they are usually very successful. Follow the advice of your veterinarian.

during these tests has a lot to do with whether or not the pup is tired from playing in the morning, what it has eaten and several other factors. Many male hunters prefer to work with female pups and female hunters like to work with male pups, so this is also a factor in how people choose their new Griff.

Training a pup or young dog for hunting includes socializing (introducing) him to all of the situations he will encounter, and potentially be afraid of or confused by, in the field. These include water, gunfire, different types of cover and terrain and, of course, birds and other game. Obviously, the pup also has to learn the recall (come) command and to retrieve as well as other basic obedience exercises.

Griff pups house-train very easily and will learn to do their "business" outside in a matter of two or three weeks. Settling down inside the house is another matter. A WPG pup is an energetic bundle of pure exploration, and an owner should take care that the tyke doesn't get into anything he shouldn't. Puppy-proofing a home is important when a Griff pup is present. Crate-training is great for this breed, although it is important to remember that the crate is not a prison but a comfortable place where the pup can go to relax.

OFA Hip Dysplasia Numbers* (1071 dogs tested)	
Excellent:	21.8%
Good:	60.7%
Fair:	9.6%
Mild:	3.6%
Moderate:	3.0%
Severe:	0.6%
*from 2003 statistics	

HEALTH CONCERNS

The WPG breed is lucky—it has relatively few genetic concerns. There are incidences of hip dysplasia, a hereditary defect of the hip joint, but responsible breeding has lowered the occurrence of the condition to 10% for the entire breed. No puppy is immune to the genetic condition, but making sure that the pup's parents have been certified as being "excellent" or "good" by the Orthopedic Foundation for Animals (OFA) or the University of Pennsylvania's Hip Improvement Program (PennHIP) is the best way to try to avoid the condition. Between "good" and "mild" hip status is a class of dogs called "fair." Some people believe that these "fair" dogs should not be bred, so use your best judgment when buying a pup.

Panosteitis, or growing pains, can sometimes affect the Griff. The long bones can become inflamed, causing pain and sudden lameness. Diagnosis is done by x-ray.

Griffs are very affectionate dogs, responding positively to loving attention and approval from their owners.

Entropion can occur in the WPG's eyelids, causing the eyelashes to rub against the sensitive tissues of the eye. This is a genetic problem and is very painful to the dog, requiring surgery to correct it. A dog affected by entropion which has been surgically corrected cannot compete in dog shows.

THE IDEAL GRIFF OWNER

The ideal owner for a WPG is an individual avid hunter or a hunting family. Many people see photos of the Griff and decide that they would love to wake up every day to that charming, woolly face. The reality is, however, that not everyone is the ideal owner for this breed, no matter how cute its fuzzy face is or how good the prospective owner's intentions are. This dog loves—and lives—to hunt. He will not be content as a house dog, nor will any amount of jogging satisfy his energy level. He needs to burn off hunting energy, not just physical energy.

Breeders are producing better, faster and more instinct-driven dogs. Bringing one of these dogs into a pet-only home is like lighting matches in a gasoline refinery. These dogs want and need to hunt. Most are only truly happy running 5 miles or more through cover each day, following scents and pointing game. This doesn't mean that you have to hunt every day—or that you have to hunt at all—but you have to allow the dog to hunt, no matter if you're going to shoot a bird or not. According to some breed enthusiasts, the WPG that isn't allowed to hunt will get flabby and soft and will lose some of his personality. The Griff is happiest when working hard.

These dogs also like to retrieve and find great pleasure in doing a good job for their owners. They are great at retrieving a ball (when there's no dead bird to bring back) and will play ball tirelessly with the kids until the kids are exhausted.

The WPG is not an apartment dog, unless that apartment is

smack in the middle of some pretty great hunting grounds. It's not a breed that will typically do well in an urban setting. It simply needs a more natural environment and plenty of space to run.

RESCUE
Even though this is a rare breed, there are some Griffs that find their way into WPG rescue organizations. These dogs are in need of good, permanent homes. They are often older dogs and may have some behavioral issues to contend with. This doesn't mean that a rescued dog won't make a great pet or hunter. On the contrary, many rescued dogs excel at every lesson, simply happy to have a kind owner and a warm home. Beware, however, that some rescued Griffs might not get along with cats or other pets that may effect a prey-driven response.

A rescued Griff might not come with registration papers, but you can petition the AKC for an ILP (Indefinite Listing Privilege) number for your spayed or neutered dog, allowing the dog to compete for obedience, agility, hunting, tracking and Junior Showmanship titles.

A multi-Griff household can be lots of fun—if you have the room and the time.

BREED STANDARD FOR THE

WIREHAIRED POINTING GRIFFON

The breed standard for the Wirehaired Pointing Griffon is the "blueprint" by which all WPGs are judged. Breeders aspire to have their puppies meet this standard as closely as possible. The standard considers the appearance of the dog as well as the movement and temperament. If a dog is to compete in conformation shows, he must conform to this standard. The WPG that wins any conformation show is the dog in the ring which the judge believes to be the closest to the standard. The dogs aren't really competing against each other—they are being compared to this standard and measured against it.

The American Kennel Club (AKC) registers over one million

Dog in profile showing typical shaggy outline with correct type, balance and structure of an active hunter.

dogs each year, sponsors over 15,000 shows and trials held by their licensed and member clubs and works diligently to support the breeders, exhibitors and judges who make the dog sport happen. The parent club for the WPG is the American Wirehaired Pointing Griffon Association, and it is the standard of the AWPGA, as adopted by the AKC, that we present here. Following the AKC standard is the French working standard for the breed, established in 1984, which details the breed's hunting style and is a reference for fanciers around the world.

AKC STANDARD FOR THE WIREHAIRED POINTING GRIFFON

General Appearance: Medium sized, with a noble, square-shaped head, strong of limb, bred to cover all terrain encountered by the walking hunter. Movement showing an easy catlike gracefulness. Excels equally as a pointer in the field, or a retriever in the water. Coat is hard and coarse, never curly or woolly, with a thick undercoat of fine hair, giving an unkempt appearance. His easy trainability, devotion to family and friendly temperament endear him to all. The nickname of "supreme gundog" is well earned.

Size, Proportion, Substance: *Size*—22 to 24 inches for males, 20 to 22 inches for females. Correct size is important. Oversize to be severely penalized. *Proportion*—Slightly longer than tall, in a ratio of 10 to 9. Height from withers to ground; length from point of shoulder to point of buttocks. The Griffon must not evolve towards a square conformation. Substance medium, reflecting his work as an all-terrain hunting dog.

Head: The head is to be in proportion to the overall dog. The *skull* is of medium width with equal length from nose to stop and from stop to occiput. The skull is slightly rounded on top, but from the side the *muzzle* and head are square. The *stop*

Head study featuring typical ragamuffin appearance and proper structure, type and proportion.

and *occiput* are only slightly pronounced. The required abundant mustache and eyebrows contribute to the friendly expression. The *eyes* are large and well open, more rounded than elliptical. They have an alert, friendly and intelligent expression. Eye color ranges in all shades of yellow and brown. Haws should not show nor should there be protruding eyes. The ears should be of medium size, lying flat and close to the head, set high, at the height of the eye line. *Nose*—Well open nostrils are essential. Nose color is always brown. Any other color is a disqualification. *Bite*—Scissors. Overshot or undershot bite is a serious fault.

Neck, Topline, Body: *Neck*—Rather long, slightly arched, no dewlap. *Topline*—The back is strong and firm, descending in a gentle slope from the slightly higher withers to the base of the tail. *Chest*—The chest must descend to the level of the elbow, with a moderate spring of rib. The chest must neither be too wide nor too narrow, but of medium width to allow freedom of movement. The loin is strong and well developed, being of medium length. The croup and rump are stoutly made with adequate length to favor speed. The *tail* extends from the back in a continuation of the topline. It may be carried straight or raised slightly. It is docked by one-third to one-half length.

Forequarters: Shoulders are long, with good angulation and well laid back. The forelegs are straight and vertical from the front and set well under the shoulder from the side. Pasterns are slightly sloping. Dewclaws should be removed. Feet are round, firm, with tightly closed webbed toes. Pads are thick.

BETTER THAN THE AVERAGE DOG

Even though you may never show your dog, you should still read the breed standard. The breed standard tells you more than just physical specifications such as how tall your dog should be; it also describes how he should act, how he should move and what unique qualities make him the breed that he is. You are not investing money in a pure-bred dog so that you can own a dog that "sort of looks like" the breed you're purchasing. You want a typical, handsome representative of the breed, one that all of your friends and family and people you meet out in public will recognize as the breed you've so carefully selected and researched. If the parents of your prospective puppy bear little or no resemblance to the dog described in the breed standard, you should keep searching!

Hindquarters: The thighs are long and well muscled. Angulation in balance with the front. The legs are vertical with the hocks turning neither in nor out. The stifle and hock joints are strong and well angulated. Feet as in front.

Coat: The coat is one of the distinguishing features of the breed. It is a double coat. The outer coat is medium length, straight and wiry, never curly or woolly. The harsh texture provides protection in rough cover. The obligatory undercoat consists of a fine, thick down, which provides insulation as well as water resistance. The undercoat is more or less abundant, depending upon the season, climate and hormone cycle of the dog. It is usually lighter in color. The head is furnished with a prominent mustache and eyebrows. These required features are extensions of the undercoat, which gives the Griffon a somewhat untidy appearance. The hair covering the ears is fairly short and soft, mixed with longer harsh hair from the coat. The overall feel is much less wiry than the body. The legs, both front and rear, are covered with denser, shorter and less coarse hair. The coat on the tail is the same as the body; any type of plume is prohibited. The breed should be exhibited in full

FAULTS IN PROFILE

Ewe-necked, soft topline, low tail set, generally lacking bone and substance, weak and straight behind, flat feet, long back.

Upright shoulders, high withers, kink in tail, straight behind, high in the rear.

Short neck, upright shoulders, narrow front, toes out in front, poor tail carriage, weak rear lacking correct angulation.

Short thick neck, upright and loaded shoulders, weak pasterns and flat feet, sloping topline and lacking angulation behind.

body coat, not stripped short in pattern. Trimming and stripping are only allowed around the ears, top of head, cheeks and feet.

Color: Preferably steel gray with brown markings, frequently chestnut brown, or roan, white and brown; white and orange also acceptable. A uniformly brown coat, all white coat or white and orange are less desirable. A black coat disqualifies.

Gait: Although close working, the Griffon should cover ground in an efficient, tireless manner. He is a medium-speed dog with perfect coordination between front and rear legs. At a trot, both front and rear legs tend to converge toward the center line of gravity. He shows good extension both front and rear. Viewed from the side, the topline is firm and parallel to the line of motion. A smooth, powerful ground-covering ability can be seen.

"Alert, friendly and intelligent" describe the Griff's expressive eyes, and this dog's sweet look couldn't fit the bill better.

Temperament: The Griffon has a quick and intelligent mind and is easily trained. He is outgoing, shows a tremendous willingness to please and is trustworthy. He makes an excellent family dog as well as a meticulous hunting companion.

Disqualifications: Nose any color other than brown. Black coat.

Approved October 8, 1991
Effective November 28, 1991

FRENCH WORKING STANDARD FOR THE WIREHAIRED POINTING GRIFFON

The general running style (the manner in which a dog crosses a course, including speed and efficiency) of the Griffon is that of a galloper, with a slight rocking movement from front to rear around the center of gravity. The feline pace, supple and skimming gallop is characteristic. Its length (specific to midlines), back rectitude, slanting shoulders and angled hocks give this type of run pace, intermitting phases of trot are tolerated but not desired. The gallop must be situated in the continental style but it must be rapid, energetic and maintained.

The quartering must be daring and extended as long as the dog stays within the control of the handler. (The dog is generally working into the wind). The head must be carried at least in a straight line or higher with the back. The head is carried slightly forward and tilted down, forming an angle with the neck, called hammer bearing. However, scent working and gliding near the game must be done nose up. Tracking is not permitted, because working the nose down, except in special events is done against the wind (blood-retrieving).

In the point position, the head must be in the extension of the line of the spine. The body must be rigid, neck extended, the limbs slightly bent. The pointing style of the Griffon should be half down, but stopping dead in his tracks is acceptable. The dog may be close to or on the ground, tail rigid and motionless. When the point is taken at a distance, the dog must approach as near as possible to the game, situating and blocking it before it flushes. It is the relocation of the dog. This approach action, called "roading," must be done in a feline style, the body lower toward the ground, the limbs bent, the nose up. Dog crouches more and more the closer he gets to the game. He may end up crawling flat on his belly for the point. This action must be done with avid determination.

Translation provided by Jacques Carpentier, former Vice President of the Club Français du Griffon d'Arrêt a Poil Dur Korthals, courtesy of the AWPGA.

YOUR PUPPY

WIREHAIRED POINTING GRIFFON

SELECTING YOUR GRIFF PUP

There's no real science in selecting a good WPG puppy. Most experts in the breed say that you will have just as much luck randomly pulling a good puppy out of a litter as you would if choosing after hanging around all day watching the pups.

Of course, you want to make sure that you're buying your Griff from a reputable breeder, one that comes with recommendations from the parent club. If you want your Griff for hunting, it would be a good idea to buy a pup whose parents are superb hunters. If you want a great conformation dog, try to find a pedigreed pup whose parents have attained their championships.

Many male hunters like to hunt with female Griffs, and many female hunters like to work with male Griffs. It's commonly thought that male dogs get along better with women and female dogs with men. There may be some truth to this adage, though it is more likely a function of how the human relates to the dog in question.

The health of the parents plays a role in the health of your future pup. Make sure that the parents have received a "good" to "excellent" rating on the test for hip dysplasia. For more information on this, check out the Orthopedic Foundation for Animals at www.offa.org or the PennHIP program at www.pennhip.org.

If you are able to see the parents of your potential puppy, do so. Ask about their temperament, and watch how they interact with the humans and other dogs around them. The puppies themselves should be outgoing and appreciative of

Don't choose on cuteness alone. Choose an active and alert puppy who is interested in getting to know you.

human attention. They should not be fearful, snappish (which is different from puppy play-nipping) or lethargic. However, you may have gotten to the breeder's house just after the pups have played themselves to exhaustion and they might be sleeping. Don't turn away a good WPG pup just because he is tired when you go to visit.

FINDING A FIELD PUPPY

For potential owners of field dogs, the advice from a professional gundog trainer is second to none when it comes to finding the right kind of breeder who consistently produces top-quality working dogs. When purchasing a field puppy, visit a few kennels and spend time observing the breeder's dogs working in the field. They should exhibit catlike grace, smooth ground-covering movement and superb coordination, all virtues of this athletic hunting breed. You can trust that the breeder is producing consistent workers, so it is not essential to buy a puppy from the dogs you are watching in the field, but be sure that they are from the same lines. Ask the

REGISTERING YOUR WPG PUPPY

The United Kennel Club (UKC) and the American Kennel Club (AKC) are the country's two largest all-breed registries. Selecting a registry depends on what the new owner's intentions with his WPG are. If he wishes to show the dog in an AKC dog show, then purchasing the dog from AKC-registered parents is essential. If the owner wishes to participate in field trials held by the American Field or hunting tests held by the National Shoot to Retrieve Association (NSTRA), then he must abide by the rules of that organization. Investigating the various registries and clubs online will yield valuable information.

The American Field is the country's oldest registry, established in 1874. It registers kennel names, records field trial wins and publishes a newsletter that includes current registrations. The Field Dog Stud Book provides registration certificates as well as certified pedigrees to all dogs registered. They are based in Chicago and can be contacted online at www.americanfield.com.

NSTRA serves as a registry as well as the sponsor of field trials for all pointing dogs, promoting fairness between all pointing breeds and excellent trial quality. Membership inquiries and puppy registrations can be done online at www.nstra.org. The organization is located in Plainfield, Indiana.

The North American Versatile Hunting Dog Association (NAVHDA) is organized to serve the needs of hunters in North America, fostering and improving hunting breeds in the US and promoting game conservation. NAVHDA's activities and services complement those of other registries and field trial clubs.

WIREHAIRED POINTING GRIFFON

Tug-of-war. Puppies learn the rules of the pack through games with littermates.

breeder for references so you can talk to other owners who shoot over his dogs.

Another avenue to finding a well-bred field prospect is to contact a professional gundog trainer. Such an individual can steer you in the right direction so that the puppy you start with has the most advantages possible. When selecting a puppy for the field, owners often look for ancestors' accomplishments in field trials, and even though this isn't a guarantee of ability in the pups, it's a terrific start. As long as you are purchasing a puppy from a proven line, you can be reasonably sure that the puppy you get will have the desired prey drive and natural ability to work. The pup's genealogy promises that it will have ability to run swiftly, follow scent and handle the stress of the actual hunt. Additionally, a well-bred puppy will have a stronger desire to please you, an important characteristic of the Griffon breed.

TEMPERAMENT ABOVE ALL ELSE

Regardless of breed, a puppy's disposition is perhaps his most important quality. It is, after all, what makes a puppy lovable and "livable." If the puppy's parents or grandparents are known to be snappy or aggressive, the puppy is likely to inherit those tendencies. That can lead to serious problems, such as the dog's becoming a biter, which can lead to eventual abandonment.

Your Puppy

A COMMITTED NEW OWNER

By now you should understand what makes the Wirehaired Pointing Griffon a most unique and special dog, one that may fit nicely into your family and lifestyle, especially if you are a hunting enthusiast and live in a nice country setting. If you have researched breeders, you should be able to recognize a knowledgeable and responsible WPG breeder who cares not only about his pups but also about what kind of owner you will be. You will likely not find a Griff breeder who is going to sell you a "pet-only" Griff puppy, even if it's the runt of the litter. You have to be serious about this breed, or you'll break the puppy's heart and maybe your own as well.

As mentioned, a visit with the puppies and their breeder can be an education in itself, though nothing is guaranteed with the Griff. Breed research, breeder selection and puppy visitation are very important aspects of finding the puppy of your dreams. Puppy personalities within each litter vary, from the shy and easygoing puppy to the one who is dominant and assertive, with most pups falling somewhere in between. You may be able to learn the differences from one pup to the next by spending time with the puppies, but you can't bank on these observations. Griff breeders will tell you many stories about how the shy, laid-back puppy turned out to be a field champion or how the wild and crazy puppy transformed into a polite show dog or house companion (who also hunts on weekends). The breeder can give you his input, which is certainly valuable, and the rest is a roll of the dice. As long as all of the puppies are healthy, sound and responsive, you might as well just follow your heart.

GETTING ACQUAINTED

When visiting a litter, ask the breeder for suggestions on how best to interact with the puppies. If possible, get right into the middle of the pack and sit down with them. Observe which pups climb into your lap and which ones shy away. Toss a toy for them to chase and bring back to you. It's easy to fall in love with the first puppy who picks you, but keep your future objectives in mind before you make your final decision.

CRATE EXPECTATIONS

To make the crate more inviting to your puppy, you can offer his first meal or two inside the crate, always keeping the crate door open so that he does not feel confined. Keep a favorite toy or two in the crate for him to play with while inside. You can also cover the crate at night with a lightweight sheet to make it more den-like and remove the stimuli of household activity. Never put him into his crate as punishment or as you are scolding him, since he will then associate his crate with negative situations and avoid going there.

The decision to live with a WPG is a serious commitment and not one to be taken lightly. A Griff will change your life: your commitment to this living, sentient and very active being is a life-altering event. This puppy now depends on you for his basic survival, including his food, water, shelter and protection, not to mention his exercise. Of course, the new pup needs love, nurturing and a proper canine education to mold him into a responsible, well-behaved canine citizen. Your WPG's health and good manners will need consistent monitoring and regular "tune-ups," so your job as a responsible dog owner will be ongoing throughout every stage of his life.

Although the responsibilities of owning a dog may at times tax your patience, the joy of living with your Wirehaired Pointing Griffon far outweighs the workload, and a well-mannered adult dog is worth your time and effort. Before your very eyes, your new charge will grow up to be your most loyal friend, devoted to you unconditionally.

YOUR WPG SHOPPING LIST

Just as expectant parents prepare a nursery for their baby, so should you ready your home for the arrival of your Griff pup. If you have the necessary puppy supplies purchased and in place before he comes home, it will ease the puppy's transition from the warmth and familiarity of his mom and littermates to the brand-new environment of his new home and human family. You will

Your Puppy

be too busy to stock up and prepare your house after your pup comes home, that's for sure. Imagine how a pup must feel upon being transported to a strange new place. It's up to you to comfort him and to let your little pup know that he is going to be happy with you.

FOOD AND WATER BOWLS

Your puppy will need separate bowls for his food and water. Stainless steel pans are generally preferred over plastic bowls since they sterilize better and pups are less inclined to chew on the metal. Heavy-duty ceramic bowls are popular, but consider how often you will have to pick up those heavy bowls. Buy adult-sized pans, as your puppy will grow into them before you know it.

A Griff needs bowls that are sturdy, easy to clean and indestructible. Stainless steel is the answer for the Griff.

THE DOG CRATE

If you think that crates are tools of punishment and confinement for when a dog has misbehaved, think again. Nearly all experienced Griffon breeders and trainers recommend a crate as the preferred house-training aid as well as for all-around puppy training and safety. Because dogs are natural den creatures that prefer cave-like environments, the benefits of crate use are many. The crate provides the puppy with his very own "safe house," a cozy

These Griff puppies know that the crate is nothing to be afraid of.

COST OF OWNERSHIP

The purchase price of your puppy is merely the first expense in the typical dog budget. Quality dog food, veterinary care (sickness and health maintenance), dog supplies and grooming costs will add up to big bucks every year. Can you adequately afford to support a canine addition to the family?

place to sleep, take a break or seek comfort with a favorite toy; a travel aid to house your dog when on the road, at motels or at the vet's office; a training aid to help teach your puppy proper toileting habits; and a place of solitude when non-dog people happen to drop by and don't want a lively puppy—or even a well-behaved adult dog—saying hello or begging for attention.

Crates come in several types, although the wire crate and the fiberglass airline-type crate are the most popular. Both are safe and your puppy will adjust to either one, so the choice is up to you. The wire crates offer better visibility for the pup as well as better ventilation. Many of the wire crates easily collapse into suitcase-size carriers. The fiberglass crates, similar to those used by the airlines for animal transport, are sturdier and more den-like. However, the fiberglass crates do not collapse and are less ventilated than a wire crate; this can be problematic in hot weather. Some of the newer crates are made of heavy plastic mesh; they are very lightweight and fold up into slim-line suitcases. However, a mesh crate might not be suitable for a pup with manic chewing habits.

Don't bother with a puppy-sized crate. Although your Griffon puppy will be a little fellow when you bring him home, he will grow up in the blink of an eye and your puppy crate will be useless. Purchase a crate that will accommodate an adult WPG. He will stand about 24 inches at the shoulder when fully grown, so a large-sized crate will be needed.

> **CREATE A SCHEDULE**
> Puppies thrive on sameness and routine. Offer meals at the same time each day, take him out at regular times for potty trips and do the same for play periods and outdoor activity. Make note of when your puppy naps and when he is most lively and energetic, and try to plan his day around those times. Once he is house-trained and more predictable in his habits, he will be better able to tolerate changes in his schedule.

Crate-trained puppies are more amenable to confinement whenever the need arises, such as travel, the vet's office, the grooming salon, etc.

Your Puppy

A cozy place to cuddle will make your Griff puppy comfortable in his new home.

BEDDING AND CRATE PADS

Your puppy will enjoy some type of soft bedding in his "room" (the crate), something he can snuggle into to feel cozy and secure. Old towels or blankets are good choices for a young pup, since he may (and probably will) have a toileting accident or two in the crate or decide to chew on the bedding material. Once he is fully trained and out of the early chewing stage, you can replace the puppy bedding with a permanent crate pad if you prefer. Crate pads and other dog beds run the gamut from inexpensive to high-end doggie-designer styles, but don't splurge on the good stuff until you are sure that your puppy is reliable and won't tear it up or make a mess on it.

PUPPY TOYS

Just as infants and older children require objects to stimulate their minds and bodies, puppies need toys to entertain their curious brains, wiggly paws and achy teeth. A fun array of safe doggie toys will help satisfy your puppy's chewing instincts and distract him from gnawing on the leg of your antique chair or your new leather sofa. Most puppy toys are cute and look as if they would be a lot of fun, but not all are necessarily safe or good for your puppy, so use caution when you go puppy-toy shopping.

Although WPGs are not known to be voracious chewers like many other dogs, they still love to chew. The best "chewcifiers" are nylon and hard rubber bones, which are safe to gnaw on and come in sizes appropriate for all age groups and breeds. Be especially careful of natural bones, which can splinter or develop dangerous sharp edges; pups can easily swallow or choke on those bone splinters.

Even a young pup will show signs very early on of the hunting and retrieving instinct of the breed.

TOYS 'R SAFE

The vast array of tantalizing puppy toys is staggering. Stroll through any pet shop or pet-supply outlet and you will see that the choices can be overwhelming. However, not all dog toys are safe or sensible. Most very young puppies enjoy soft woolly toys that they can snuggle with and carry around. (You know they have outgrown them when they shred them up!) Avoid toys that have buttons, tabs or other enhancements that can be chewed off and swallowed. Soft toys that squeak are fun, but make sure your puppy does not disembowel the toy and remove (and swallow) the squeaker. Toys that rattle or make noise can excite a puppy, but they present the same danger as the squeaky kind and so require supervision. Hard rubber toys that bounce can also entertain a pup, but make sure that the toy is too big for your pup to swallow.

Veterinarians often tell of surgical nightmares involving bits of splintered bone, because in addition to the danger of choking, the sharp pieces can damage the intestinal tract.

Similarly, rawhide chews, while a favorite of most dogs and puppies, can be equally dangerous. Pieces of rawhide are easily swallowed after they get soft from chewing, and dogs have been known to choke on pieces of ingested rawhide. Rawhide chews should be offered only when you can supervise the puppy.

Soft woolly toys are special puppy favorites. They come in a wide variety of cute shapes and sizes; some look like little stuffed animals. Puppies love to shake them up and toss them about or simply carry them around. Be careful of fuzzy toys that have button eyes or noses that your pup could chew off and swallow, and make sure that he does not disembowel a squeaky toy to remove the squeaker! Braided rope toys are similar in that they are fun to chew and toss around, but they shred easily and the strings are easy to swallow. The strings are not digestible, and if the puppy doesn't pass them in his stool, he could end up at the vet's office. As with rawhides, your puppy should be closely monitored with rope toys.

If you believe that your pup has ingested one of these

Your Griff puppy won't let you forget that he's a bird-dog-in-training!

dangerous objects, check his stool for the next couple of days to see if he passes the item when he defecates. At the same time, also watch for signs of intestinal distress. A call to your veterinarian might be in order to get his advice and be on the safe side.

An all-time favorite toy for puppies (young and old!) is the empty gallon milk jug. Hard plastic juice containers—46 ounces or more—are also excellent. Such containers make lots of noise when they are batted about, and puppies go crazy with delight as they play with them. However, they don't often last very long, so be sure to remove and replace them when they get chewed up.

COLLARS

A lightweight nylon collar is the best choice for a very young pup. Quick-click collars are easy to put on and remove, and they can be adjusted as the puppy grows. Introduce him to his collar as soon as he comes home to get him accustomed to wearing it. He'll get used to it quickly and won't mind a bit. Make sure that it is snug enough that it won't slip off yet loose enough to be comfortable for the pup. You should be able to slip two fingers between the collar and his neck. Check the collar often, as puppies grow in spurts, and his collar can become

The profuse, wiry coat of the Griff can make the dog's collar tight and uncomfortable. Check the collar regularly for correct fit.

FIRST CAR RIDE
The ride to your home from the breeder will no doubt be your puppy's first automobile experience, and you should make every effort to keep him comfortable and secure. Bring a large towel or small blanket for the puppy to lie on during the trip and an extra towel in case the pup gets carsick or has a potty accident. It's best to have another person with you to hold the puppy in his lap. Most puppies will fall fast asleep from the rolling motion of the car. If the ride is lengthy, you may have to stop so that the puppy can relieve himself, so be sure to bring a leash and collar for those stops. Avoid rest areas for potty trips, since those are frequented by many dogs, who may carry parasites or disease. It's better to stop at grassy areas near gas stations or shopping centers to prevent unhealthy exposure for your pup.

COLLARING OUR CANINES

The standard flat collar with a buckle or a snap, in leather, nylon or cotton, is widely regarded as the everyday all-purpose collar. If the collar fits correctly, you should be able to fit two fingers between the collar and the dog's neck.

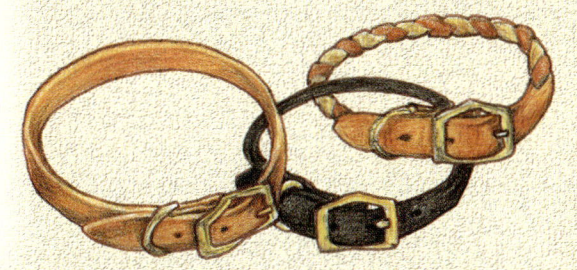

Leather Buckle Collars

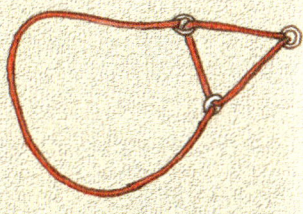

Limited-Slip Collar

The martingale, Greyhound or limited-slip collar is preferred by many dog owners and trainers. It is fixed with an extra loop that tightens when pressure is applied to the leash. The martingale collar gets tighter but does not "choke" the dog. The limited-slip collar should only be used for walking and training, not for free play or interaction with another dog. These types of collar should never be left on the dog, as the extra loop can lead to accidents.

Choke collars, usually made of stainless steel, are made for training purposes but are not recommended for small dogs or heavily coated breeds. The chains can injure small dogs or damage long/abundant coats. Thin nylon choke leads are commonly used on show dogs while in the ring, though they are not practical for everyday use.

Snap-Bolt Choke Collar

The harness, with two or three straps that attach over the dog's shoulders and around his torso, is a humane and safe alternative to the conventional collar. By and large, a well-made harness is virtually escape-proof. Harnesses are available in nylon and mesh and can be outfitted on most dogs, ranging in chest girths of from 10 to 30 inches.

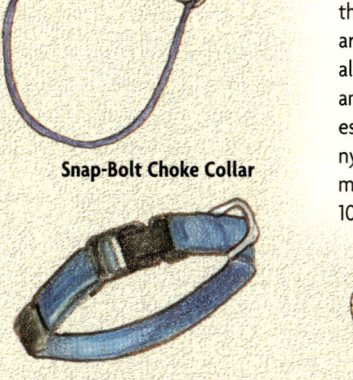

Harness

Nylon Collar

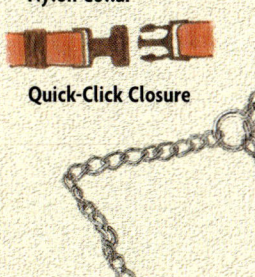

Quick-Click Closure

Snake Chain

Chrome Steel

Fur-Saver

Choke Chain Collars

A head collar, composed of a nylon strap that goes around the dog's muzzle and a second strap that wraps around his neck, offers the owner better control over his dog. This device is recommended for problem-solving with dogs (including jumping up, pulling and aggressive behaviors) but must be used with care.

A training halter, including a flat collar and two straps, made of nylon and webbing, is designed for walking. There are several on the market; some are more difficult to put on the dog than others. The halter harness, with two small slip rings at each end, is recommended for ease of use.

Leash Life

Dogs love leashes! Believe it or not, most dogs dance for joy every time their owners pick up their leashes. The leash means that the dog is going for a walk—and there are few things more exciting than that! Here are some of the kinds of leashes that are commercially available.

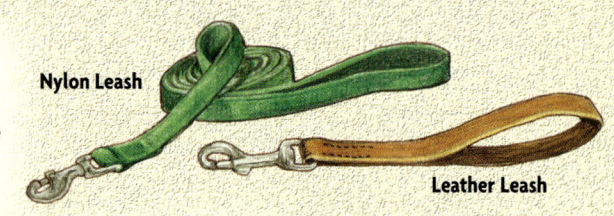

Nylon Leash

Leather Leash

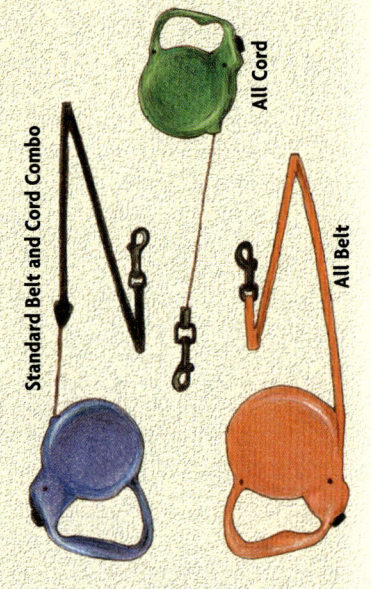

Traditional Leash: Made of cotton, nylon or leather, these leashes are usually about 6 feet in length. A quality-made leather leash is softer on the hands than a nylon one. Durable woven cotton is a popular option. Lengths can vary up to about 48 feet, designed for different uses.

Chain Leash: Usually a metal chain leash with a plastic handle. This is not the best choice for most breeds, as it is heavier than other leashes and difficult to manage.

Retractable Leash: A long nylon cord is housed in a plastic device for extending and retracting. This leash, also known as a flexible leash, is ideal for taking trained dogs for long walks in open areas, although it is not always suitable for large, powerful breeds. Different lengths and sizes are available, so check that you purchase one appropriate for your dog's weight.

Elastic Leash: A nylon leash with an elastic extension. This is useful for well-trained dogs, especially in conjunction with a head halter.

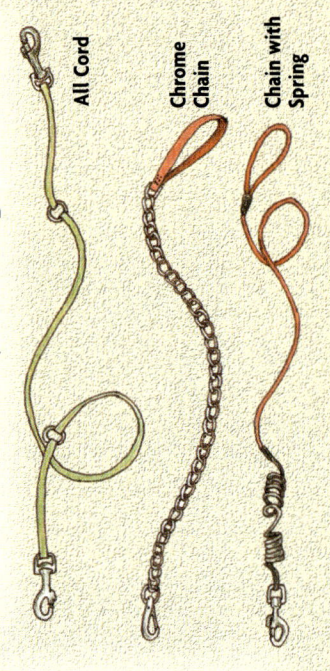

Standard Belt and Cord Combo / All Cord / All Belt

Retractable Leashes

All Cord / Chrome Chain / Chain with Spring

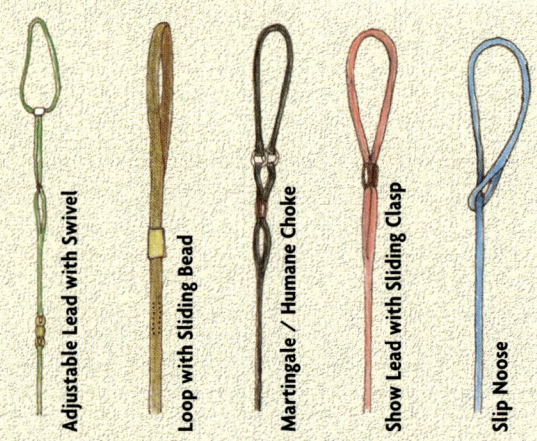

Avoid leashes that are completely elastic, as they afford minimal control to the handler.

Adjustable Leash: This has two snaps, one on each end, and several metal rings. It is handy if you need to tether your dog temporarily, but is never to be used with a choke collar.

Tab Leash: A short leash (4 to 6 inches long) that attaches to your dog's collar. This device serves like a handle, in case you have to grab your dog while he's exercising off lead. It's ideal for "half-trained" dogs or dogs that listen only half of the time.

Slip Leash: Essentially a leash with a collar built in, similar to what a dog-show handler uses to show a dog. This British-style collar has a ring on the end so that you can form a slip collar. Useful if you have to catch your own runaway dog or a stray.

Adjustable Lead with Swivel / Loop with Sliding Bead / Martingale / Humane Choke / Show Lead with Sliding Clasp / Slip Noose

A Variety of Collar-Leash-in-One Products

Your Puppy

too tight almost overnight. Choke collars are for training purposes only and should never be used on young puppies.

Leashes
A 6-foot nylon lead is an excellent choice for a young puppy. It is lightweight and not as tempting to chew as a leather lead. You can switch to a 6-foot leather lead after your pup has grown and is used to walking politely on a lead. For initial puppy walks and house-training purposes, you should invest in a shorter lead so that you have more control over the puppy. At first, you don't want him wandering too far away from you, and when taking him out for toileting you will want to keep him in the specific area chosen for his potty spot.

Once the puppy is heel-trained with a traditional leash, you can consider purchasing a retractable lead. A retractable lead (appropriate to your adult dog's weight) is excellent for walking dogs that are already leash-wise. This type of lead allows the dog to roam farther away from you and explore a wider area when out walking and also retracts when you need to keep him close.

There is a wide variety of leashes from which to choose. For the athletic WPG, purchase a strong and sturdy leash. Quality pet products are a necessity when you own a gundog like the WPG.

TOXIC PLANTS
Plants are natural puppy magnets, but many can be harmful, even fatal, if ingested by a puppy or adult dog. Scout your yard and home interior and remove any plants, bushes or flowers that could be even mildly dangerous. It could save your puppy's life. You can obtain a complete list of toxic plants from your veterinarian, at the public library or by looking online.

Hide and seek! Curiosity defines the WPG puppy. You must be diligent in supervising your little dynamo at all times.

HOME SAFETY FOR YOUR PUP

The importance of puppy-proofing cannot be overstated. In addition to making your house comfortable for your WPG's arrival, you also must make sure that your house is safe for your puppy before you bring him home. There are countless hazards in the owner's personal living environment that a pup can sniff, chew, swallow or destroy. Many are obvious; others are not. Do a thorough advance house check to remove or rearrange those things that could hurt your puppy, keeping any potentially dangerous items out of areas to which he will have access.

Electrical cords are especially dangerous, since puppies view them as irresistible chew toys. Unplug and remove all exposed cords or fasten them beneath baseboards where the puppy cannot reach them. Veterinarians and firefighters can tell you horror stories about electrical burns and house fires that resulted from puppy-chewed electrical cords. Consider this a most serious precaution for your puppy and the rest of your family.

Scout your home for tiny objects that might be seen at a pup's eye level. Keep medication bottles and cleaning supplies well out of reach, and do the same with waste baskets and other trash containers. It goes without saying that you should not use rodent poison or other toxic chemicals in any puppy area and that you must keep such containers safely locked up. You will be amazed at how many places a curious puppy can discover!

A Dog-Safe Home

The dog-safety police are taking you and your new puppy on a house tour. Let's go room by room and see how safe your own home is for your new pup. The following items are doggy dangers, so either they must be removed or the dog should be monitored or not allowed access to these areas.

Outdoors
- swimming pool
- pesticides
- toxic plants
- lawn fertilizers

Living Room
- house plants (some varieties are poisonous)
- fireplace or wood-burning stove
- paint on the walls (lead-based paint is toxic)
- lead drapery weights (toxic lead)
- lamps and electrical cords
- carpet cleaners or deodorizers

Bathroom
- blue water in the toilet bowl
- medicine cabinet (filled with potentially deadly bottles)
- soap bars, bleach, drain cleaners, etc.
- tampons

Kitchen
- household cleaners in the kitchen cabinets
- glass jars and canisters
- sharp objects (like kitchen knives, scissors and forks)
- garbage can (with remnants of good-smelling things like onions, potato skins, apple or pear cores, peach pits, coffee beans and other harmful tidbits)
- food left out on counters (some foods are toxic to dogs)

Garage
- antifreeze
- fertilizers (including rose foods)
- pesticides and rodenticides
- pool supplies (chlorine and other chemicals)
- oil and gasoline in containers
- sharp objects, electrical cords and power tools

ARE VACCINATIONS NECESSARY?

Vaccinations are recommended for all puppies by the American Veterinary Medical Association (AVMA). Some vaccines are absolutely necessary, while others depend upon a dog's or puppy's individual exposure to certain diseases or the animal's immune history. Rabies vaccinations are required by law in all 50 states. Some diseases are fatal whereas others are treatable, making the need for vaccinating against the latter questionable. Follow your veterinarian's recommendations to keep your dog fully immunized and protected. You can also review the AVMA directive on vaccinations on their website: www.avma.org.

Once your house has cleared inspection, check your yard. A sturdy fence, well embedded into the ground, will give your dog a safe place to play and potty. Although WPGs are not known to be climbers or fence jumpers, they are still athletic dogs, so a 6-foot-high fence should be adequate to contain an agile youngster or adult. Check the fence periodically for necessary repairs. If there is a weak link or space to squeeze through, you can be sure a determined WPG will discover it.

The garage and shed can be hazardous places for a pup, as things like fertilizers, chemicals and tools are usually kept there. It's best to keep these areas off limits to the pup. Antifreeze is especially dangerous to dogs, as they find the taste appealing and it takes only a few licks from the driveway to kill a dog, puppy or adult, small breed or large.

VISITING THE VETERINARIAN

A good veterinarian is your Griff puppy's best health-insurance policy. If you do not already have a vet, ask dog-experienced friends in your area for recommendations so that you can select a vet before you bring your WPG puppy home. Also arrange for your puppy's first veterinary examination beforehand, since many vets have waiting periods and your puppy should visit the vet within a day or so of coming home.

Your Puppy

Puppies that grow up with children form a special bond with their human "siblings."

It's important to make sure your puppy's first visit to the vet is a pleasant and positive one. The vet should take great care to befriend the pup and handle him gently to make their first meeting a positive experience. The vet will give the pup a thorough physical examination and set up a schedule for vaccinations and other necessary wellness visits. Be sure to show your vet any health and inoculation records, which you should have received from your breeder. Your vet is a great source of canine health information, so be sure to ask questions and take notes. Creating a health journal for your puppy will make a handy reference for his wellness and any future health problems that may arise.

MEETING THE FAMILY

Your WPG's homecoming is an exciting time for all members of the family, and it's only natural that everyone will be eager to meet him, pet him and play with him. However, for the puppy's sake, it's best to make these initial family meetings as uneventful as possible so that the pup is not overwhelmed with too much too soon. Remember, he has just left his dam and his littermates and is

Hands-on socialization reinforces the human-animal bond. A few belly rubs and soon you will be the center of your Griff's universe.

his new crate during this first day home. Toss a treat or two inside the crate; if he associates the crate with food, he will associate the crate with good things. If he is comfortable with the crate, you can offer him his first meal inside it. Leave the door ajar so he can wander in and out as he chooses.

FIRST NIGHT IN HIS NEW HOME

So much has happened in your WPG puppy's first day away from the breeder. He's had his first car ride to his new home. He's met his new human family and perhaps the other family pets. He has explored his new house and yard, at least those places where he is to be allowed during his first away from the breeder's home for the first time. Despite his fuzzy wagging tail, he is still apprehensive and wondering where he is and who all these strange humans are. It's best to let him explore on his own and meet the family members as he feels comfortable. Let him investigate all the new smells, sights and sounds at his own pace. Children should be especially careful to not get overly excited, use loud voices or hug the pup too tightly. Be calm, gentle and affectionate, and be ready to comfort him if he appears frightened or uneasy.

Be sure to show your puppy

THE CRITICAL SOCIALIZATION PERIOD

Canine research has shown that a puppy's 8th through 16th week is the most critical learning period of his life. This is when the puppy "learns to learn," a time when he needs positive experiences to build confidence and stability. Puppies who are not exposed to different people and situations outside the home during this period can grow up to be fearful and sometimes aggressive. This is also the best time for puppy lessons, since he has not yet acquired any bad habits that could undermine his ability to learn.

Your Puppy

weeks at home. He may have visited his new veterinarian. He has eaten his first meal or two away from his dam and littermates. Surely that's enough to tire out a young Griff pup—or so you hope!

It's bedtime. During the day the pup investigated his crate, which is his new den and sleeping space, so it is not entirely strange to him. Line the crate with a soft towel or blanket that he can snuggle into and gently place him into the crate for the night. Some breeders send home a piece of bedding from where the pup slept with his littermates, and those familiar scents are a great comfort for the puppy on his first night without his siblings.

He will probably whine or cry. The puppy is objecting to the confinement and the fact that he is alone for the first time. This can be a stressful time for you as well as for the pup. It's important that you remain strong and don't let

Early socialization and interaction with the breeder and littermates are a good head start in life for any puppy.

the puppy out of his crate to comfort him. He will fall asleep eventually. If you release him, the puppy will learn that crying means "out" and will continue that habit. You are laying the groundwork for future habits. Some breeders find that soft music can soothe a crying pup and help him get to sleep.

SOCIALIZING YOUR PUPPY
The first 20 weeks of your Griff puppy's life are the most important of his entire lifetime. A properly socialized puppy will grow up to be a confident and stable adult who will be a pleasure to live with and a welcome addition to the neighborhood.

The importance of socialization cannot be overemphasized. Research on canine behavior has proven that puppies who are not exposed to new sights, sounds, people and animals during their first 20 weeks of life will grow up to be timid and fearful, even aggressive, and unable to flourish outside of their home environment.

Socializing your puppy is not difficult and, in fact, will be a fun time for you both. Lead training goes hand in hand with socialization, so your puppy will be learning how to walk on a lead at the same time that he's meeting the neighborhood. Because the WPG is such a remarkable breed, everyone will enjoy meeting "the new Griff on the block." Surely you'll have to tell everyone who meets him that he is not a German Wirehaired Pointer. You might also volunteer that he's not a Cesky Fousek either! Take him for short walks to the park and to other dog-friendly places where he will encounter new people, especially children. Puppies automatically recognize children as "little people" and are drawn to play with them. Just make sure that you supervise these meetings and that the children do not get too rough or encourage him to play too hard. An overzealous

Meeting the litter can be very exciting if not a bit overwhelming. Prepare yourself with a list of questions for the breeder before arriving at the kennel.

pup can often nip too hard, frightening the child and in turn making the puppy overly excited. A bad experience in puppyhood can impact a dog for life, so a pup that has a negative experience with a child may grow up to be shy or even aggressive around children.

Take your puppy along on your daily errands. Puppies are natural "people magnets," and most people who see your pup will want to pet him. All of these encounters will help to mold him into a confident adult dog.

Be especially careful of your puppy's encounters and experiences during the eight-to-ten-week-old period, which is also called the "fear period." This is a serious imprinting period, and all contact during this time should be gentle and positive. A frightening or negative event could leave a permanent impression that could affect his future behavior if a similar situation arises.

Also make sure that your puppy has received his first and second rounds of vaccinations before you expose him to other dogs or bring him to places that other dogs may frequent. Avoid dog parks and other strange-dog areas until your vet assures you that your puppy is fully immunized and resistant to the diseases that can be passed between canines. Discuss socialization with your breeder, as some breeders recommend socializing the puppy even before he has received all of his inoculations, depending on how outgoing the puppy may be.

LEADER OF THE PUPPY'S PACK

Like other canines, your puppy needs an authority figure, someone he can look up to and regard as the leader of his "pack." His first pack leader was his dam, who taught him to be polite and not chew too hard on her ears or

Your puppy may think he is the "cock of the walk," but be sure to establish who the pack leader is from the very beginning—you!

nip at her muzzle. He learned those same lessons from his littermates. If he played too rough, they cried in pain and stopped the game, which sent an important message to the rowdy puppy.

As puppies play together, they are also struggling to determine who will be the boss. Being pack animals, dogs need someone to be in charge. If a litter of puppies remained together beyond puppyhood, one of the pups would emerge as the strongest one, the one who calls the shots.

Once your puppy leaves the pack, he will look intuitively for a new leader. If he does not recognize you as that leader, he will try to assume that position for himself. Of course, it is hard to imagine your fuzzy Griff puppy trying to be in charge when he is so small and seemingly helpless. You must remember that these are natural canine instincts. Do not cave in and allow your pup to get the upper "paw," but never be harsh with the Griff, who does not respond to strong-handed training methods.

Just as socialization is so important during these first 20 weeks, so too is your puppy's early education. He was born without any bad habits. He does not know what is good or bad behavior. If he does things like nipping and digging, it's because he is having fun and doesn't know that humans consider these things as "bad." It's your job to teach him proper puppy manners, and this is the best time to accomplish that—before he has developed bad habits, since it is much more difficult to "unlearn" or correct unacceptable learned behavior than to teach good behavior from the start.

> **BE CONSISTENT**
> Consistency is a key element, in fact is absolutely necessary, to a puppy's learning environment. A behavior (such as chewing, jumping up or climbing onto the furniture) cannot be forbidden one day and then allowed the next. That will only confuse the pup, and he will not understand what he is supposed to do. Just one or two episodes of allowing an undesirable behavior to "slide" will imprint that behavior on a puppy's brain and make that behavior more difficult to erase or change.

A pup can learn a lot from the older dogs in the "pack," and you can learn from watching a pup and adult interact.

Make sure that all members of the family understand the importance of being consistent when training their new puppy. If you tell the puppy to stay off the sofa and your daughter allows him to cuddle on the couch to watch her favorite television show, your pup will be confused about what he is and is not allowed to do. Have a family conference before your pup comes home so that everyone understands the basic principles of puppy training and the rules you have set forth for the pup, and agrees to follow them.

The old saying that "an ounce of prevention is worth a pound of cure" is especially true when it comes to puppies. It is much easier to prevent inappropriate behavior than it is to change it. It's also easier and less stressful for the pup, since it will keep discipline to a minimum and create a more positive learning environment for him. That, in turn, will also be easier on you.

SOLVING PUPPY PROBLEMS

CHEWING AND NIPPING

Nipping at fingers and toes is normal puppy behavior. Chewing is also the way that puppies investigate their surroundings. However, you will have to teach your puppy that chewing anything other than his toys is not acceptable. That won't happen overnight and at times puppy teeth will test your patience. However, if you allow nipping and chewing to continue, just think about the damage that a mature WPG can do with a full set of adult teeth.

Whenever your puppy nips your hand or fingers, cry out "Ouch!" in a loud voice, which should startle your puppy and stop him from nipping, even if only for a moment. Immediately distract him by offering a small treat or an appropriate toy for him to chew instead (which means having chew toys and puppy treats handy or in your pockets at all times). Praise him when he takes the toy and tell him what a good fellow he is. Praise is just as or even more important in puppy training as discipline and correction.

The orally fixated Griff puppy will think just about anything is chew-worthy; you must nip this bad behavior in the bud.

There's so much you can teach your Griff to do, but it is highly unlikely that this sporting breed is interested in self-grooming.

Puppies also tend to nip at children more often than adults, since they perceive little ones to be more vulnerable and more similar to their littermates. Teach your children appropriate responses to nipping behavior. If they are unable to handle it themselves, you may have to intervene. Puppy nips can be quite painful and a child's frightened reaction will only encourage a puppy to nip harder, which is a natural canine response. As with all other puppy situations, interaction between your WPG puppy and children should be supervised.

Chewing on objects, not just family members' fingers and ankles, is also normal canine behavior that can be especially tedious (for the owner, not the pup) during the teething period when the puppy's adult teeth are coming in. At this stage, chewing just plain feels good. Furniture legs and cabinet corners are common puppy favorites. Shoes and other personal items also taste pretty good to a pup.

The best solution is, once again, prevention. If you value something, keep it tucked away and out of reach. You can't hide your dining-room table in a closet, but you can try to deflect the chewing by applying a bitter product made just to deter dogs from chewing. This spray-on substance is vile-tasting, although safe for dogs, and most puppies will avoid the forbidden object after one tiny taste. You also can apply the product to your leather leash if the puppy tries to chew on his lead during leash-training sessions.

Keep a ready supply of safe chews handy to offer your WPG as a distraction when he starts to chew on something that's a "no-

ESTABLISH A ROUTINE
Routine is very important to a puppy's learning environment. To facilitate house-training, use the same exit/entrance door for potty trips and always take the puppy to the same place in the yard. The same principle of consistency applies to all other aspects of puppy training.

no." Remember, at this tender age, he does not yet know what is permitted or forbidden, so you have to be "on call" every minute he's awake and on the prowl.

You may lose a treasure or two during your puppy's growing-up period, and the furniture could sustain a nasty nick or two. These can be trying times, so be prepared for those inevitable accidents and comfort yourself in knowing that this too shall pass.

JUMPING UP
Although WPG pups are not known to be notorious jumpers, they are still puppies after all, and puppies jump up—on you, your guests, your counters and your furniture. Just another normal part of growing up, and one you need to meet head-on before it becomes an ingrained habit.

The key to jump correction is consistency. You cannot correct your WPG for jumping up on you today, then allow it to happen tomorrow by greeting him with hugs and kisses. As you have learned by now, consistency is critical to all puppy lessons.

For starters, try turning your back as soon as the puppy jumps. Jumping up is a means of gaining your attention, and if the pup can't see your face, he may get discouraged and learn that he loses eye contact with his beloved master when he jumps up.

Leash corrections also work, and most puppies respond well to a leash tug if they jump. Grasp the leash close to the puppy's collar and give a quick tug downward, using the command "Off." Do not use the word "Down," since "Down" is used to teach the puppy to lie down, which is a separate action that he will learn during his education in the basic commands. As soon as the puppy has backed off, tell him to sit and immediately praise him for doing so. This will take many repetitions and won't be accomplished quickly, so don't get discouraged or give up; you must be even

Be consistent when training your Griff; if you don't want him jumping up on strangers, friends and family members, you shouldn't allow him to jump up on you.

more persistent than your puppy.

A second method used for jump correction is the spritzer bottle. Fill a spray bottle with water mixed with a bit of lemon juice or vinegar. As soon as the puppy jumps, command him "Off" and spritz him with the water mixture. Of course, that means having the spray bottle handy whenever or wherever jumping usually happens.

Yet a third method to discourage jumping is grasping the puppy's paws and holding them gently but firmly until he struggles to get away. Wait a brief moment or two, then release his paws and give him a command to sit. He should eventually learn that jumping gets him into an uncomfortable predicament.

Children are major victims of puppy jumping, since puppies view little people as ready targets for jumping up as well as nipping. If your children (or their friends) are unable to dispense jump corrections, you will have to intervene and handle it for them.

Important to prevention is also knowing what you should not do. Never kick your WPG (for any reason, not just for jumping) or knock him in the chest with your knee. That maneuver could actually harm your puppy. Vets can tell you stories about puppies who suffered broken bones after being banged about when they jumped up.

PUPPY WHINING

Puppies often cry and whine, just as infants and little children do. It's their way of telling us that they are lonely or in need of attention. Your puppy will miss his littermates and will feel insecure when he is left alone. You may be out of the house or just in another room, but he will still feel alone. During these times, the puppy's crate should be his personal comfort station, a place all his own where he can feel safe and secure. Once he learns that being alone is okay and not something to be feared,

If you and the Griff are a compatible match, you'll find that the addition of a pup will bring much joy.

Your Puppy

he will settle down without crying or objecting. You might want to leave a radio on while he is crated, as the sound of human voices can be soothing and will give the impression that people are around.

Give your puppy a favorite cuddly toy or chew toy to entertain him whenever he is crated. You will both be happier: the puppy because he is safe in his den and you because he is quiet, safe and not getting into puppy escapades that can wreak havoc in your house or cause him danger.

To make sure that your puppy will always view his crate as a safe and cozy place, never, ever use the crate as punishment. That's the best way to turn the crate into a negative place that the pup will want to avoid. Sure, you can use the crate for your own peace of mind if your puppy is getting into trouble and needs some "time out." Just don't let him know that! Never scold the pup and immediately place him into the crate. Count to ten, give him a couple of hugs and maybe a treat, then scoot him into his crate.

It's also important not to make a big fuss when he is released from the crate. That will make getting out of the crate more appealing than being in the crate, which is just the opposite of what you are trying to achieve.

A wiry-coated bundle of Griff puppy love.

PROPER CARE OF YOUR
WIREHAIRED POINTING GRIFFON

FEEDING THE WPG
Most owners feed puppy food to the WPG until the pup is between 6 and 12 months of age. Feed only a high-quality food. Because this breed is relatively free of health problems, it doesn't need any particular formula of food the way some other breeds might, but it still needs a food with a high nutrient value per serving. Dry kibble is the most appropriate food for an adult Griff.

Many owners opt to free-feed their dogs, which means leaving a bowl of kibble out all day for the dog to graze whenever he likes. This is absolutely the wrong feeding approach for the WPG. It is extremely important not to free-feed the Griff. When you offer a couple of meals a day, you become the source of the food, which is much better for training. Free-feeding can also

Mother's milk provides the puppies with what they need for the healthiest start in life.

HOLD THE ONIONS
Sliced, chopped, grated; dehydrated, boiled, fried or raw; pearl, Spanish, white or red: onions can be deadly to your dog. The toxic effects of onions in dogs are cumulative for up to 30 days. A serious form of anemia, called Heinz body anemia, affects the red blood cells of dogs that have eaten onions. For safety (and better breath), dogs should avoid chives and scallions as well.

cause bloat or obesity, because some dogs do not know when to stop eating. Bloat can be deadly and obesity can cause diabetes, joint problems and kidney and liver damage.

Consult your veterinarian or the back of the bag of kibble for feeding amounts. Remember to offer more food when the dog is hunting frequently. The more exercise your dog gets, the more food he will need. Some owners even double the portions when a dog is working particularly hard.

Treats are fine in moderation and are particularly good to use during training, though some owners prefer not to use treats during training, feeling that the dog should perform for performance's sake, not for a tidbit.

If your veterinarian suggests switching to a senior formula for your older Griff, then do so, but most owners do not change the diet, regardless of the dog's age.

Skin allergies caused by a dog's diet can be a problem in some individuals, though this is not common. There are allergy formulas available that may help your dog with this problem.

WATER AT ALL TIMES
For a thirsty Griff, it's always time for a drink! Regardless of

Your breeder should give you diet suggestions and feeding instructions to take home with your new puppy.

VARIETY IS THE SPICE
Although dog-food manufacturers contend that dogs don't like variety in their diets, studies show quite the opposite to be true. Dogs would much rather vary their meals than eat the same old chow day in and day out. Dry kibble is no more exciting for a dog than the same bowl of bran flakes would be for you. Fortunately, there are dozens of varieties available on the market, and your dog will likely show preference for certain flavors over others. A word of warning: don't overdo it or you'll develop a fussy eater who only prefers chopped beef fillet and asparagus tips every night.

QUENCHING HIS THIRST

Is your dog drinking more than normal and trying to lap up everything in sight? Excessive drinking has many different causes. Obvious causes for a dog's being thirstier than usual are hot weather and vigorous exercise. However, if your dog is drinking more for no apparent reason, you could have cause for concern. Serious conditions like kidney or liver disease, diabetes and various types of hormonal problems can all be indicated by excessive drinking. If you notice your dog's being excessively thirsty, contact your vet at once. Hopefully there will be a simpler explanation, but the earlier a serious problem is detected, the sooner it can be treated, with a better rate of cure.

what type of food he eats, there's no doubt that he needs plenty of water, and he'll happily splash it all over the house. Fresh cold water, in a clean bowl, should be freely available to your dog at all times. There are special circumstances, such as during puppy housebreaking, when you will want to monitor your pup's water intake so that you will be able to predict when he will need to relieve himself, but water must be available to him nonetheless. Water is essential for hydration and proper body function just as it is in humans.

You will get to know how much your dog typically drinks in a day. Of course, in the heat or if exercising vigorously, he will be more thirsty and will drink more. However, if he begins to drink noticeably more water for no apparent reason, this could signal any of various problems, and you are advised to consult your vet.

A word of caution concerning your deep-chested dog's water intake: he should never be allowed to gulp water, especially at mealtimes. In fact, his water intake should be limited at mealtimes as a rule. This simple daily precaution can go a long way in protecting your dog from the dangerous and potentially fatal gastric torsion (bloat).

What Is "Bloat" and How Do I Prevent it?

You likely have heard the term "bloat," which refers to gastric torsion (gastric dilatation/volvulus), a potentially fatal condition. As it is directly related to feeding and exercise practices, a brief explanation here is warranted. The term *dilatation* means that the dog's stomach is filled with air, while *volvulus* means that the stomach is twisted around on itself, blocking the entrance/exit points. Dilatation/volvulus is truly a deadly combination, although they also can occur independently of each other. An affected dog cannot digest food or pass gas, and blood cannot flow to the stomach, causing accumulation of toxins and gas along with great pain and rapidly occuring shock.

Many theories exist on what exactly causes bloat, but we do know that deep-chested breeds are more prone. Activities like eating a large meal, gulping water, strenuous exercise too close to mealtimes or a combination of these factors can contribute to bloat, though not every case is directly related to these more well-known causes. With that in mind, we can focus on incorporating simple daily preventives and knowing how to recognize the symptoms. In addition to the tips presented in this book, ask your vet about how to prevent and recognize bloat. An affected dog needs immediate veterinary attention, as death can result quickly. Signs include obvious restlessness/discomfort, crying in pain, drooling/excessive salivation, unproductive attempts to vomit or relieve himself, visibly bloated appearance and collapsing. Do not wait: get to the vet *right away* if you see any of these symptoms. The vet will confirm by x-ray if the stomach is bloated with air; if so, the dog must be treated *immediately*.

As varied as the causes of bloat are the tips for prevention, but some common preventive methods follow:
- Feed two or three small meals daily rather than one large one;
- Do not feed water before, after or with meals, but allow access to water at all other times;
- Never permit rapid eating or gulping of water;
- No exercise for the dog at least two hours before and (especially) after meals;
- Feed high-quality food with adequate protein, adequate fiber content and not too much fat and carbohydrate;
- Explore herbal additives, enzymes or gas-reduction products (only under a vet's advice) to encourage a "friendly" environment in the dog's digestive system;
- Avoid foods and ingredients known to produce gas;
- Avoid stressful situations for the dog, especially at mealtimes;
- Make dietary changes gradually, over a period of a few weeks;
- Do not feed dry food only;
- Although the role of genetics as a causative of bloat is not known, many breeders do not breed from previously affected dogs;
- Sometimes owners are advised to have gastroplexy (stomach stapling) performed on their dogs as a preventive measure;
- Pay attention to your dog's behavior and any changes that could be symptomatic of bloat. Your dog's life depends on it!

WIREHAIRED POINTING GRIFFON

Known as the "supreme gundog," the Griff can do it all, whether in the snow, in the water or in the field. He needs plenty of opportunity to exercise his body and mind.

Proper Care

Hunting activities of all kinds, both in water and on land, can play an important role in your WPG's exercise regimen. If not allowed hunting activity on a regular basis, your Griff needs an appropriate substitute.

EXERCISE FOR THE ACTIVE GRIFF

The WPG needs a great deal of exercise, as do most of the other sporting dogs. He will languish in a home where he is not provided with the right kind and amount of exercise. All the walking and jogging in the world is not enough for the WPG. This breed needs to run itself as it would on a hunt. The ideal situation for a WPG is in a hunting family where the dog is used regularly and is allowed to run off leash in a safe place on the days he's not hunting.

The WPG definitely needs a large fenced yard, ideally one that's escape-proof and includes somewhere for the dog to swim, even if it's only a children's

WIREHAIRED POINTING GRIFFON

A Griff working the field is a spectacular site, and exercise like this is an absolute necessity for this sporting breed.

Your Griff will enjoy free-running time in a securely enclosed area.

wading pool. This is a dog that loves to retrieve, so playing ball or fetch with a stick for hours is on his list of favorite things to do. Though jogging isn't the ideal exercise for a Griff, he does make a terrific jogging partner because of his high stamina and desire to please you. However, it's important not to jog a young Griff, as this can cause his bones and joints undue stress and damage.

TWO'S COMPANY

One surefire method of increasing your adult dog's exercise plan is to adopt a second dog. If your dog is well socialized, he should take to his new canine pal in no time and soon the two will be giving each other lots of activity and exercise as they play, romp and explore together. Most owners agree that two dogs are hardly much more work than one. If you cannot afford a second dog, get together with a friend or neighbor who has a well-trained dog. Your dog will definitely enjoy the company of a new four-legged playmate.

Proper Care 71

A WPG that doesn't get enough exercise can get flabby and will most likely develop temperament problems as well. This dog may become destructive of property in an effort to alleviate boredom and might not behave as the mellow house dog that he should be.

The bottom line is this: exercise your Griff! If you can find a safe place to hike where your dog is allowed off leash, try to use that spot a few times a week. If you live in a more urban environment, a couple of hours at your local dog park a few times a week should suffice, though it isn't the ideal situation for a Griff, a breed that lives to run and hunt.

GROOMING YOUR GRIFF

The WPG's coat is an all-terrain, easy-care, all-weather double coat. The ideal Griff has a harsh, wirehaired outer coat, a soft, insulating undercoat and protective furnishings around the face (eyebrows and beard). The coat varies greatly from litter to litter and from dog to dog, much to the chagrin of breeders. Some coats are too soft and some are too short and lack much of an undercoat. It is the one element of the Griff that hasn't remained consistent, even after more than 100 years of selective breeding.

The Griff's coat matures at about two years of age and changes during the course of the dog's life. A pregnant female may lose much of her coat and its luster but will regain it once the pups are weaned. The coat also changes seasonally, and some dogs "blow the coat" seasonally, though this is not common to the Griff in general.

A rousing romp with other Griffs is a great way for your dog to release some of that sporting energy.

Nothing can compare to a properly trained and cared-for Griff on a hunt.

Brush sensitive areas like the facial furnishings gently. Don't neglect any part of the body.

A pin brush can be used after a day of hunting to remove anything the Griff may have picked up along the way.

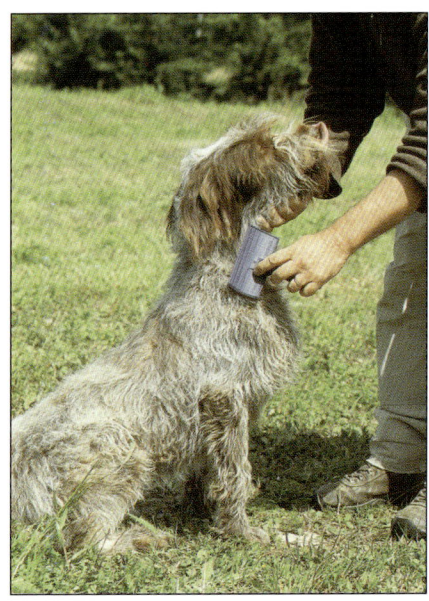

This dog will shed a little, but most hunting dogs will have their coat naturally "stripped" by dense cover while on a hunt. If not, hand-stripping (called "rolling the coat") is recommended. Simply pull the dead hair out with your thumb and forefinger, pulling in the direction the coat grows and not against it. Stripping with a "stripping knife" is another technique. Pulling out the hair might seem cruel, but the dogs actually seem to enjoy it. Remember to pull only a few hairs at a time. Do not grab a hunk of coat and try to pull it out. Grooming should be a fun experience for both you and your dog, and another opportunity to bond. Ask your breeder or a friend who has grooming experience to show you the basic technique if you're unsure.

Along with stripping, conformation Griffs will also get a bit of clipping, but most hunters don't clip the coat, leaving it instead to protect the dog from the elements. It is traditional in the United States to have a shaggy Griff, while in Europe they prefer them a little more kempt. If you do scissor or clip the coat, make sure to be conservative with the facial furnishings, as these are very slow to grow out again. In any case, whatever you do, don't strip or clip your Griff so that it looks as if you've done just that, as with other wirehaired breeds. The

Proper Care

overall look of the Griff should be unshorn and shaggy.

A good coat with a balance of wiry hair and undercoat should not need much brushing, perhaps once or twice a month to make sure that no mats form. Some owners use a wire comb or pin brush, ideally one that will get down through the thick undercoat. Brushing should ideally happen after a hunt or a hardy romp through vegetation. The dog is likely to pick up burs, twigs and perhaps even ticks. It's a good idea to go over the dog quickly with a brush (or your hands) to make sure there's nothing hitching a ride in the coat.

The WPG is not known to have a doggy smell, so he shouldn't need regular bathing. In fact, most hunters never bathe their dogs. Unless the dog gets into something particularly stinky, like rolling in a long-dead animal or having a run-in with a skunk, the dog should not need to be bathed. The regularity of bathing is a personal choice.

The ears are of particular importance during grooming. They are prone to infection because the Griff has a lot of hair in his ears. The hair is easily pulled out, and most dogs actually enjoy the experience. Be careful to never scissor inside the ears! Always pull the hair out with a professional tool like a hemostat. Some owners use an ear powder or an ear solution to keep the ears clean and dry. If you smell a foul or yeasty odor coming

The area around the eyes and the facial furnishings can be spot-cleaned with a damp soft cloth.

The ears should be cleaned with a soft cotton ball or wipe. Never probe into the ear canal.

WIREHAIRED POINTING GRIFFON

between the pads on the underside of the foot.

Check the teeth and gums regularly too. Make sure nothing is stuck in the gums (you never know what a Griff can get into!) and make sure that there's no tartar build-up. You can brush your Griff's teeth with special flavored toothpaste for dogs and a special finger brush. Your veterinarian can also do regular teeth scaling while the dog is under anesthesia for another procedure.

Begin grooming your Griff puppy immediately, so that he gets used to all of the different sensations of being groomed. The earlier you begin, the easier it will be for you or a groomer to neaten up your beautiful beast.

Accustom the puppy to nail clipping from a young age. With a little encouragement, puppies accept manicures without too much fuss.

from the ears, or notice a sticky substance inside of them, consult your veterinarian. This could indicate an infection or some type of mite infestation.

The nails should be clipped regularly. If they are left to grow too long, the dog may develop foot, leg and gait problems. You can use a regular dog nail clipper (found in any pet shop) or an electric grinder (Dremel tool). Make sure to cut as much as you can off the nail without cutting into the "quick," which will cause the nail to bleed. In case the nail does bleed, have some styptic powder on hand to stop the bleeding immediately. While you're clipping the nails, take this opportunity to neaten up the feet as well. Trim the hair from

Checking and cleaning your dog's teeth is an essential facet of his proper healthcare. Many serious problems can stem from a lack of effective dental care.

PET OR STRAY?

Besides the obvious benefit of providing your contact information to whoever finds your lost dog, an ID tag makes your dog more approachable and more likely to be recovered. A strange dog wandering the neighborhood without a collar and tags will look like a stray, while the collar and tags indicate that the dog is someone's pet. Even if the ID tags become detached from the collar, the collar alone will make a person more likely to pick up the dog.

IDENTIFICATION AND TRAVEL

PROPER ID FOR YOUR WPG

You love your Griffon and want to keep him safe. Of course you take every precaution to prevent his escaping from the yard or becoming lost or stolen. You have a sturdy high fence and you always keep your dog on lead when out and about in public places. If your dog is not properly identified, however, you are overlooking a major aspect of his safety. We hope to never be in a situation where our dog is missing, but we should practice prevention in the unfortunate case that this happens; identification greatly increases the chances of your dog's being returned to you.

There are several ways to identify your dog. First, the traditional dog tag should be a staple in your dog's wardrobe, attached to his everyday collar. Tags can be made of sturdy plastic and various metals and should include your contact information so that a person who finds the dog can get in touch with you right away to arrange his return. Many people today enjoy the wide range of decorative tags available, so have fun and create a tag to match your dog's personality. Of course, it is important that the tag stays on the collar, so have a secure attachment; hunters often prefer the type of tag that slides right onto the collar.

In addition to the ID tag, which every dog should wear even if identified by another method, two other forms of identification have become popular: microchipping and tattooing. In microchipping, a tiny scannable chip is painlessly inserted under the dog's skin. The number is

It's a big world out there, and if your WPG is not properly identified, you are neglecting a major aspect of proper dog care.

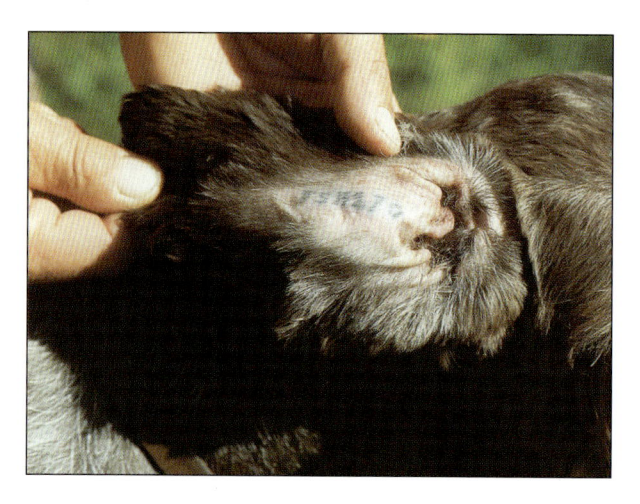

Tattooing is a permanent method of ID that works best when the tattoo is placed in a visible area on the dog.

registered to you so that, if your lost dog turns up at a clinic or shelter, the chip can be scanned to retrieve your contact information.

The advantage of the microchip is that it is a permanent form of ID, but there are some factors to consider. Several different companies make microchips, and not all are compatible with the others' scanning devices. It's best to find a company with a universal microchip that can be read by scanners made by other companies as well. It won't do any good to have the dog chipped if the information cannot be retrieved. Also, not every humane society, shelter and clinic is equipped with a scanner, although more and more facilities are equipping themselves. In fact, many shelters microchip dogs that they adopt out to new homes.

In the US, there are five or six major microchip manufacturers as well as a few databases, such as the American Kennel Club's Companion Animal Recovery unit and HomeAgain™ Companion Animal Retrieval System (Schering-Plough). In the UK, The Kennel Club is affiliated with the National Pet Register, operated by Wood Green Animal Shelters.

Because the microchip is not visible to the eye, the dog must wear a tag that states that he is microchipped so that whoever picks him up will know to have him scanned. He of course also should have a tag with your contact information in case his chip cannot be read. Humane societies and veterinary clinics offer this service, which is usually very affordable.

YOUR PACK ANIMAL

If you are bringing your dog along with you on a vacation, here's a list of the things you want to pack for him:
- leashes (conventional and retractable)
- collar with ID tag
- dog food and bottled water
- grooming tools
- flea and tick preventatives
- crate and crate pad
- pooper-scooper and plastic bags
- toys and treats
- towels and paper towels
- first-aid kit
- dog license and rabies certificate

Proper Care

Though less popular than microchipping, tattooing is another permanent method of ID for dogs. Most vets perform this service, and there are also clinics that perform dog tattooing. This is also an affordable procedure and one that will not cause much discomfort for the dog. It is best to put the tattoo in a visible area, such as the ear, to deter theft. It is sad to say that there are cases of dogs' being stolen and sold to research laboratories, but such laboratories will not accept tattooed dogs.

To ensure that the tattoo is effective in aiding your dog's return to you, the tattoo number must be registered with a national organization. That way, when someone finds a tattooed dog, a phone call to the registry will quickly match the dog with his owner.

Your Griffs will want to go everywhere with you; it is up to you to make it as comfortable and safe as possible for the dogs regardless of the means of travel.

HIT THE ROAD

Car travel with your Griff may be limited to necessity only, such as trips to the vet, or you may bring your dog along almost everywhere you go. This will depend much on your individual dog and how he reacts to rides in the car. You can begin desensitizing your dog to car travel as a pup so that it's something that he's used to. Still, some dogs suffer from motion sickness. Your vet may prescribe a medication for this if trips in the car pose a problem for your dog. At the very least, you will need to get him to the vet, so he will need

Some dogs are born travelers and will jump at the chance to go for a drive.

WIREHAIRED POINTING GRIFFON

Even with the windows open, leaving a dog alone in a car is not a good idea, as the dog can hurt himself trying to get out or he could even be stolen.

to tolerate these trips with the least amount of hassle possible.

Start taking your pup on short trips, maybe just around the block to start. If he is fine with short trips, lengthen your rides a little at a time. Start to take him on your errands or just for drives around town. By this time it will be easy to tell whether your dog is a born traveler or would prefer staying at home when you are on the road.

Of course, safety is a concern

Make stops for potty and water breaks and to let your Griff stretch his legs.

THE STROKE OF 106

When traveling with your dog in the summer months, never leave the dog unattended in the car, even if the car is parked in the shade. A dog can suffer from heat prostration or sunstroke after just a few minutes. In summer heat, dogs must always have access to water, a cool resting place and ventilation.

You can identify heatstroke by the following signs: panting, gasping for air, weakness, collapse, deep red gums and uncontrolled movement or seizures. The dog's body temperature could rise to 105–110 degrees F. If you recognize these signs, here's a quick first-aid lesson. Submerge the dog in cool water if his temperature is 105 degrees or greater. Continue to cool the dog's body, including his head and neck, for at least 30 minutes, monitoring his temperature every 2 or 3 minutes. Stop the cooling process once the dog's temperature reaches 103 degrees, as it will continue to descend and you don't want it to go below normal (around 101.5 degrees). Take the dog to the vet, because shock or other temperature changes can occur even after the critical period has ended.

for dogs in the car. First, he must travel securely, not left loose to roam about the car where he could be injured or distract the driver. A young pup can be held by a passenger initially but should soon graduate to a travel crate, which can be the same crate he uses in the home. Other options include a car harness (like a seat belt for dogs) and partitioning the back of the car with a gate made for this purpose.

Bring along what you will need for the dog. He should wear his collar and ID tags, of course, and you should bring his leash, water (and food if a long trip) and clean-up materials for potty breaks and in case of motion sickness. Always keep your dog on his leash when you make stops, and never leave him alone in the car. Many a dog has died from the heat inside a closed car; this does not take much time at all. A dog left alone inside a car can also be a target for thieves.

FLY ME TO THE MOON

Taking a trip by air does not mean that your dog cannot accompany you, it just means that you will have to be well informed and well prepared. The majority of dogs travel as checked cargo; only the smallest of breeds are allowed in the cabin with their owners. Your dog must travel in an airline-approved travel crate appropriate to his size so that he will be safe and comfortable during the flight. If

> **DON'T LEAVE HOME WITHOUT IT!**
>
> For long trips, there's no doubt that the crate is the safest way to travel with your dog. Luckily, there are some other options for owners who can't accommodate a crate in their cars or whose dogs prove exceptionally difficult to crate-train. In some states, seatbelts are mandatory for humans, and you can consider using the seatbelt on your dog. Purchase a safety harness made for passenger pooches and pull your car's seatbelt through the loop on the harness.
>
> Larger dogs can be restrained in the rear of the vehicle with a barrier, which you can purchase from a pet store or pet-supply outlet. The barrier is constructed of aluminum, steel or mesh netting. While this device will keep the dog in a designated area, it will not protect him from being jostled about the vehicle on a bumpy ride.

the crate that you use at home does not meet the airline's specifications, you can purchase one from the airline or from your pet-supply store (making sure it is labeled as airline-approved).

It's best to have the crate in advance of your trip to give the dog time to get accustomed to it. You can put a familiar blanket and a favorite toy or two in the crate with the dog to make him feel at home and to keep him occupied. The crate should be lined with absorbent material for the trip, with bowls for food and water attached to the outside of the crate. The crate must be labeled with your contact information, feeding instructions (where applicable), the words "Live Animal" and arrows to indicate upright position. You will also have to provide proof of current vaccinations.

Again, advance planning is the key to smooth sailing in the skies. Make your reservations well ahead of time and know what restrictions your airline imposes: no travel during certain months, refusal of certain breeds, restrictions on certain destinations, etc. You will need to follow all of the airline's rules to help your pet enjoy a safe flight.

> **DOGGONE!**
> If dogs could talk, many would say, "Take me with you!" Fortunately, more and more destinations are opening their doors to four-legged guests.
>
> Wendy Ballard is the editor and publisher of the *DogGone*™ newsletter, which comes out bi-monthly and features fun articles by dog owners who love to travel with their dogs. The newsletter includes information about fun places to go with your dogs, including popular vacation spots, dog-friendly hotels, parks, campgrounds, resorts, etc., as well as interesting activities to do with your dog, such as flyball, agility and much more. You can subscribe to the publication by contacting the publisher at PO Box 651155, Vero Beach, FL 32965-1155.

If you have to travel without your Griffs, you can be sure that they'll anxiously await your return.

DOG-FRIENDLY DESTINATIONS
When planning vacations, a question that often arises is, "Who will watch the dog?" More and more families, however, are answering that question with, "We will!" With the rise in dog-friendly places to visit, the number of families who bring their dogs along on vacation is on the rise. A search online for dog-friendly vacation spots will turn up many choices, as well as resources for owners of canine travelers. Ask others for suggestions: your vet, your breeder, other dog owners, breed club members, people at the local doggie daycare.

Traveling with your WPG means providing for his comfort and safety, and you will have to pack a bag for him just as you do for yourself (although you probably won't have liver treats in your own suitcase!). Bring his everyday items: food, water, bowls, leash and collar (with ID), brush and comb, toys, bed, crate, plus any additional accessories that he will need once you get to your vacation spot. If he takes medication, don't forget to bring it with you. If going camping or on another type of outdoor excursion, take precautions to protect your dog from ticks, mosquitoes and other pests. Above all, have a good time with your dog and enjoy each other's company.

BOARDING YOUR GRIFF
Today there are many options for dog owners who need someone to care for their dogs in certain circumstances. While many think of boarding their dogs as something to do when away on vacation, many others use the services of doggie "daycare" facilities, dropping their dogs off to spend the day while they are at work. Many of these facilities offer both long-term and daily care. Many go beyond just boarding and cater to all sorts of needs, with on-site grooming, veterinary care, training classes and even "webcams" where owners can log onto the Internet and check out what their dogs are up to. Most dogs enjoy the activity and time spent with other dogs.

Before you need to use such a service, check out the ones in your area. Make visits to see the facilities, meet the staff, discuss fees and available services and see whether this is a place where you think your dog will be happy. It is best to do your research in advance so that you're not stuck at the last minute, forced into making a rushed decision without knowing whether the kennel that you've chosen meets your standards. You also can check with your vet's office to see whether they offer boarding for their clients or can recommend a good kennel in the area.

The kennel will need to see proof of your dog's health records and vaccinations so as not to spread illness from dog to dog. Your dog also will need proper identification. Owners usually experience some separation anxiety the first time they have to leave their dog in someone else's care, so it's reassuring to know that the kennel you choose is run by experienced, caring, true dog people.

Your vet can probably recommend a local kennel in which you can board your Griff. The kennel should be clean and professionally run, with adequate space and attention for each dog.

TRAINING YOUR WIREHAIRED POINTING GRIFFON

BASIC TRAINING PRINCIPLES: PUPPY VS. ADULT

There's a big difference between training an adult dog and training a young puppy. With a young puppy, everything is new! At eight to ten weeks of age, he will be experiencing many things, and he has nothing with which to compare these experiences. Up to this point, he has been with his dam and littermates, not one-on-one with people except in his interactions with his breeder and visitors to the litter.

When you first bring the puppy home, he is eager to please you. This means that he accepts doing things your way. During the next couple of months, he will absorb the basis of everything he needs to know for the rest of his life. This early age is even referred to as the "sponge" stage. After that, for the next 18 months, it's up to you to reinforce good manners by building on the foundation that you've established. Once your puppy is reliable in basic commands and behavior and has reached the appropriate age, you may gradually introduce him to some of the interesting sports, games and activities available to pet owners and their dogs.

Raising your puppy is a family affair. Each member of the family must know what rules to set forth for the puppy and how to use the same one-word commands to mean exactly the same thing every time. Even if yours is a large family, one person will soon be considered by the pup to be the leader, the alpha person in his pack, the "boss" who must be obeyed. Often that highly

BASIC PRINCIPLES OF DOG TRAINING

1. Start training early. A young puppy is ready, willing and able.
2. Timing is your all-important tool. Praise at the exact time that the dog responds correctly. Pay close attention.
3. Patience is almost as important as timing!
4. Repeat! The same word has to mean the same thing every time.
5. In the beginning, praise all correct behavior verbally, along with treats and petting.

regarded person turns out to be the one who feeds the puppy. Food ranks very high on the puppy's list of important things! That's why your puppy is rewarded with small treats along with verbal praise when he responds to you correctly. As the puppy learns to do what you want him to do, the food rewards are gradually eliminated and only the praise remains. If you were to keep up with the food treats, you could have two problems on your hands—an obese dog and a beggar.

Training begins the minute your WPG puppy steps through the doorway of your home, so don't make the mistake of putting the puppy on the floor and telling him by your actions to "Go for it! Run wild!" Even if this is your first puppy, you must act as if you know what you're doing: be the boss. An uncertain pup may be terrified to move, while a bold one will be ready to take you at your word and start plotting to destroy the house! Before you collected your puppy, you decided where his own special place would be, and that's where to put him when

A Griff puppy is like a sponge, ready to soak up all that you have to offer him. Saturate him with knowledge when he's still young.

OUR CANINE KIDS

"Everything I learned about parenting, I learned from my dog." How often adults recognize that their parenting skills are mere extensions of the education they acquired while caring for their dogs. Many owners refer to their dogs as their "kids" and treat their canine companions like real members of the family. Surveys indicate that a majority of dog owners talk to their dogs regularly, celebrate their dogs' birthdays and purchase Christmas gifts for their dogs. Another survey shows that dog owners take their dogs to the veterinarian more frequently than they visit their own physicians.

you first arrive home. Give him a house tour after he has investigated his area and had a nap and a bathroom "pit stop."

It's worth mentioning here that if you've adopted an adult dog that is completely trained to your liking, lucky you! You're off the hook! However, if that dog spent his life up to this point in a kennel, or even in a good home but without any real training, be prepared to tackle the job ahead. A dog three years of age or older with no previous training cannot be blamed for not knowing what he was never taught. While the dog is trying to understand and learn your rules, at the same time he has to unlearn many of his previously self-taught habits and general view of the world.

Working with a professional trainer will speed up your progress with an adopted adult dog. You'll need patience, too. Some new rules may be close to impossible for the dog to accept. After all, he's been successful so far by doing everything his way! (Patience again.) He may agree with your instruction for a few days and then slip back into his old ways, so you must be just as consistent and understanding in your teaching as you would be with a puppy. (More patience needed yet again.) Your dog has to learn to pay attention to your voice, your family, the daily routine, new smells, new sounds and, in some cases, even a new climate.

One of the most important things to find out about a newly adopted adult dog is his reaction to children (yours and others), strangers and your friends and how he acts upon meeting other dogs. If he was not socialized with dogs as a puppy, this could be a major problem. This does not mean that he's a "bad" dog, a vicious dog or an aggressive dog; rather, it means that he has no idea how to read another dog's body language. There's no way for him to tell whether the other dog is a friend or foe. Survival instinct takes over, telling him to attack first and ask questions later. This

CREATURES OF HABIT

Canine behaviorists and trainers aptly describe dogs as "creatures of habit," meaning that dogs respond to structure in their daily lives and welcome a routine. Do not interpret this to mean that dogs enjoy endless repetition in their training sessions. Dogs get bored just as humans do. Keep training sessions interesting and exciting. Vary the commands and the locations in which you practice. Give short breaks for play in between lessons. A bored student will never be the best performer in the class.

Canine Development Schedule

It is important to understand how and at what age a puppy develops into adulthood. If you are a puppy owner, consult this Canine Development Schedule to determine the stage of development your puppy is currently experiencing. This knowledge will help you as you work with the puppy in the weeks and months ahead.

Period	Age	Characteristics
First to Third	Birth to Seven Weeks	Puppy needs food, sleep and warmth and responds to simple and gentle touching. Needs mother for security and disciplining. Needs littermates for learning and interacting with other dogs. Pup learns to function within a pack and learns pack order of dominance. Begin socializing pup with adults and children for short periods. Pup begins to become aware of his environment.
Fourth	Eight to Twelve Weeks	Brain is fully developed. Pup needs socializing with outside world. Remove from mother and littermates. Needs to change from canine pack to human pack. Human dominance necessary. Fear period occurs between 8 and 12 weeks. Avoid fright and pain.
Fifth	Thirteen to Sixteen Weeks	Training and formal obedience should begin. Less association with other dogs, more with people, places, situations. Period will pass easily if you remember this is pup's change-to-adolescence time. Be firm and fair. Flight instinct prominent. Permissiveness and over-disciplining can do permanent damage. Praise for good behavior.
Juvenile	Four to Eight Months	Another fear period about seven to eight months of age. It passes quickly, but be cautious of fright and pain. Sexual maturity reached. Dominant traits established. Dog should understand sit, down, come and stay by now.

Note: These are approximate time frames. Allow for individual differences in puppies.

WPG pups can be a handful! Fair and consistent training will mold an exuberant young Griff into a well-rounded canine citizen.

words, they respond to the surface on which they are given approval to eliminate. The choice is yours (the dog's version is in parentheses): The lawn (including the neighbors' lawns)? A bare patch of earth under a tree (where people like to sit and relax in the summertime)? Concrete steps or patio (all sidewalks, garages and basement floors)? The curbside definitely calls for professional help and, even then, may not be a behavior that can be corrected 100% reliably (or even at all). If you have a puppy, this is why it is so very important to introduce your young puppy properly to other puppies and "dog-friendly" adult dogs.

HOUSE-TRAINING YOUR WPG

Dogs are tactility-oriented when it comes to house-training. In other

DAILY SCHEDULE

How many relief trips does your puppy need per day? A puppy up to the age of 14 weeks will need to go outside about 8 to 12 times per day! You will have to take the pup out any time he starts sniffing around the floor or turning in small circles, as well as after naps, meals, games and lessons or whenever he's released from his crate. Once the puppy is 14 to 22 weeks of age, he will require only 6 to 8 relief trips. At the ages of 22 to 32 weeks, the puppy will require about 5 to 7 trips. Adult dogs typically require 4 relief trips per day, in the morning, afternoon, evening and late at night.

(watch out for cars)? A small area of crushed stone in a corner of the yard (mine!)? The latter is the best choice if you can manage it, because it will remain strictly for the dog's use and is easy to keep clean.

You can start out with paper-training indoors and switch over to an outdoor surface as the puppy matures and gains control over his need to eliminate. For the naysayers, don't worry—this won't mean that the dog will soil on every piece of newspaper lying around the house. You are training him to go outside, remember?

WHEN YOUR PUPPY'S "GOT TO GO"
Your puppy's need to relieve himself is seemingly non-stop, but signs of improvement will be seen each week. From 8–10 weeks old, the puppy will have to be taken outside every time he wakes up, about 10–15 minutes after every meal and after every period of play—all day long, from first thing in the morning until his bedtime! That's a total of ten or more trips per day to teach the puppy where it's okay to relieve himself. With that schedule in mind, you can see that house-training a young puppy is not a part-time job. It requires someone to be home all day.

If that seems overwhelming or impossible, do a little planning. For example, plan to pick up your puppy at the start of a vacation period. If you can't get home in the middle of the day, plan to hire a dog-sitter or ask a neighbor to come over to take the pup outside, feed him his lunch and then take him out again about ten or so minutes after he's eaten. Also make arrangements with that or another person to be your "emergency" contact if you have to stay late on the job. Remind yourself—repeatedly—that this hectic schedule improves as the puppy gets older.

The nose knows: scent attraction is what leads a dog to his relief spot, and he usually does a bit of sniffing before he goes.

HOME WITHIN A HOME

Your WPG puppy needs to be confined to one secure, puppy-proof area when no one is able to watch his every move. Generally, the kitchen is the place of choice because the floor is washable. Likewise, it's a busy family area that will accustom the pup to a variety of noises, everything from pots and pans to the telephone, blender and dishwasher. He will also be enchanted by the smell of your cooking (and will never be critical when you burn something). A sturdy, high-sided exercise pen (also called an "ex-pen," a puppy version of a playpen) within the room of choice is a good means of confinement for a young pup. He can see out and has a certain amount of space in which to run about, but he is safe from dangerous things like electrical cords, heating units, trash baskets or open kitchen-supply cabinets. Place the pen where the puppy will not get a blast of heat or air conditioning.

In the pen, you can put a few toys, his bed (which can be his crate if the dimensions of pen and crate are compatible) and a few

A wire crate is fine for inside your home. The dog gets a full view of what is going on around him while being safely confined in his own private den.

Griff puppies are curious creatures and must have access only to areas that you deem safe and secure, both indoors and out.

TIDY BOY

Clean by nature, dogs do not like to soil their dens, which in effect are their crates or sleeping quarters. Unless not feeling well, dogs will not defecate or urinate in their crates. Crate-training capitalizes on the dog's natural desire to keep his den clean. Be conscientious about giving the puppy as many opportunities to relieve himself outdoors as possible. Reward the puppy for correct behavior. Praise him and pat him whenever he "goes" in the correct location. Even the tidiest of puppies can have potty accidents, so be patient and dedicate more energy to helping your puppy achieve a clean lifestyle.

house? It's the den connection.

In your "happy" voice, use the word "Crate" every time you put the pup into his den. If he's new to a crate, toss in a small biscuit for him to chase the first few times. At night, after he's been outside, he should sleep in his crate. The crate may be kept in his designated area at night or, if you want to be sure to hear those wake-up yips in the morning, put the crate in a corner of your bedroom. However, don't make any response whatsoever to whining or crying. If he's completely ignored, he'll settle down and get to sleep.

layers of newspaper in one small corner, just in case. A water bowl can be hung at a convenient height on the side of the ex-pen so it won't become a splashing pool for an innovative puppy. His food dish can go on the floor, next to, but not directly below, the water bowl.

Crates are something that pet owners are at last getting used to for their dogs. Wild or domestic canines have always preferred to sleep in den-like safe spots, and that is exactly what the crate provides. How often have you seen adult dogs that choose to sleep under a table or chair even though they have full run of the

A loving owner and a cozy bed will help the pup acclimate in no time.

WIREHAIRED POINTING GRIFFON

Keep a watchful eye on your little explorer.

Good bedding for a young puppy is an old folded bath towel or an old blanket, something that is easily washable and disposable if necessary ("accidents" will happen!). Never put newspaper in the puppy's crate. Also those old ideas about adding a clock to replace his mother's heartbeat, or a hot-water bottle to replace her warmth, are just that—old ideas. The clock could drive the puppy nuts, and the hot-water bottle could end up as a very soggy waterbed! An extremely good breeder would have introduced your puppy to the crate by letting two pups sleep together for a couple of nights, followed by several nights alone. How thankful you will be if you found that breeder.

Safe toys in the pup's crate or area will keep him occupied, but monitor their condition closely. Discard any toys that show signs of being chewed to bits. Squeaky parts, bits of stuffing or plastic or any other small pieces can cause intestinal blockage or possibly choking if swallowed.

PROGRESSING WITH POTTY-TRAINING
After you've taken your puppy out and he has relieved himself in the area you've selected, he can have some free time with the family as long as there is someone responsible for watching him. That doesn't mean just someone in the same room who is watching TV or busy on the computer, but one person who is doing nothing other than keeping an eye on the pup, playing with him on the floor and helping him understand his position in the pack.

This first taste of freedom will let you begin to set the house rules. If you don't want the dog on the furniture, now is the time to prevent his first attempts to jump up onto the couch. The word to use in this case is "Off," not "Down." "Down" is the word you will use to teach the down position, which is something entirely different.

Most corrections at this stage come in the form of simply distracting the puppy. Instead of telling him "No" for "Don't chew the carpet," distract the chomping puppy with a toy and he'll forget about the carpet.

As you are playing with the pup, do not forget to watch him closely and pay attention to his body language. Whenever you see him begin to circle or sniff, take the puppy outside to relieve himself. If you are paper-training, put him back into his confined area on the newspapers. In either case, praise him as he eliminates while he actually is in the act of relieving himself. Three seconds after he has finished is too late! You'll be praising him for running toward you, picking up a toy or whatever he may be doing at that moment, and that's not what you want to be praising him for. Timing is a vital tool in all dog training. Use it.

Remove soiled newspapers immediately and replace them with clean ones. You may want to take a small piece of soiled paper and place it in the middle of the new clean papers, as the scent will attract him to that spot when it's time to go again. That scent attraction is why it's so important to clean up any messes made in the house by using a product specially made to eliminate the odor of dog urine and droppings. Regular household cleansers won't do the trick. Pet shops sell the best pet deodorizers. Invest in the largest container you can find.

Scent attraction eventually will lead your pup to his chosen spot outdoors; this is the basis of outdoor training. When you take your puppy outside to relieve himself, use a one-word command

LEASH TRAINING

House-training and leash training go hand in hand, literally. When taking your WPG outside to do his business, lead him there on his leash. Unless an emergency potty run is called for, do not whisk the puppy up into your arms and take him outside. If you have a fenced yard, you have the advantage of letting the dog loose to go out, but it's better to put the dog on the leash and take him to his designated place in the yard until he is reliably house-trained. Taking the dog for a walk is the best way to house-train. The dog will associate the walk with his time to relieve himself, and the exercise of walking stimulates the dog's bowels and bladder. Dogs that are not trained to relieve themselves on a walk may hold it until they get back home, which of course defeats half the purpose of the walk.

Use potty time to reinforce proper on-leash behavior. Encourage him to walk by your side, not lag behind or pull ahead.

such as "Outside" or "Go-potty" (that's one word to the puppy) as you attach his leash. Then lead him to his spot. Now comes the hard part—hard for you, that is. Just stand there until he urinates and defecates. Move him a few feet in one direction or another if he's just sitting there looking at you, but remember that this is neither playtime nor time for a walk. This is strictly a business trip! Then, as he circles and squats (remember your timing), give him a quiet "Good dog" as praise. If you start to jump for joy, ecstatic over his performance, he'll do one of two things: either he will stop mid-stream, as it were, or he'll do it again for you—in the house—and expect you to be just as delighted!

Give him five minutes or so and, if he doesn't go in that time, take him back indoors to his confined area and try again in another ten minutes, or immediately if you see him sniffing and circling. By careful observation, you'll soon work out a successful schedule.

Accidents, by the way, are just that—accidents. Clean them up quickly and thoroughly, without comment, after the puppy has been taken outside to finish his business and then put back into his area or crate. If you witness an accident in progress, say "No!" in a stern voice and get the pup outdoors immediately. No punishment is needed. You and your puppy are just learning each

POTTY COMMAND

Most dogs love to please their masters; there are no bounds to what dogs will do to make their owners happy. The potty command is a good example of this theory. If toileting on command makes the master happy, then more power to him. Puppies will obligingly piddle if it really makes their keepers smile. Some owners can be creative about which word they will use to command their dogs to relieve themselves. Some popular choices are "Potty," "Tinkle," "Piddle," "Let's go," "Hurry up" and "Toilet." Give the command every time your puppy goes into position and the puppy will begin to associate his business with the command.

other's language, and sometimes it's easy to miss a puppy's message. Chalk it up to experience and watch more closely from now on.

CANINE ORDER OF THINGS

Discipline is a form of training that brings order to life. For example, military discipline is what allows the soldiers in an army to work as one. Discipline is a form of teaching and, in dogs, is the basis of how the successful pack operates. Each member knows his place in the pack and all respect the leader, or alpha dog. It is essential for your puppy that you establish this type of relationship, with you as the alpha, or leader. It is a form of social coexistence that all canines recognize and accept. Discipline, therefore, is never to be confused with punishment. When you teach your puppy how you want him to behave, and he behaves properly and you praise him for it, you are disciplining him with a form of positive reinforcement.

For a dog, rewards come in the form of praise, a smile, a cheerful tone of voice, a few friendly pats or a rub of the ears. Rewards are also small food treats. Obviously, that does not mean bits of regular dog food. Instead, treats are very small bits of special things like cheese or pieces of soft dog treats. The idea is to reward the dog with something very small that he can taste and swallow, providing instant positive reinforcement. If he has to take time to chew the treat, by the time he is finished he will have forgotten what he did to earn it!

Your puppy should never be physically punished. The displeasure shown on your face and in your voice is sufficient to signal to the pup that he has done something wrong. He wants to please everyone higher up on the social ladder, especially his leader, so a scowl and harsh voice will take care of the error. Growling out the word "Shame!" when the pup is caught in the act of doing something wrong is better than the repetitive "No." Some dogs hear "No" so often that they begin to think it's their name! By the way, do not use the dog's name when you're correcting him.

Initially, treats are the best way to motivate your Griff puppy into following your commands.

His name is reserved to get his attention for something pleasant about to take place.

There are punishments that have nothing to do with you. For example, your dog may think that chasing cats is one reason for his existence. You can try to stop it as much as you like but without success, because it's such fun for the dog. But one good hissing, spitting swipe of a cat's claws across the dog's nose will put an end to the game forever. Intervene only when your dog's eyeball is seriously at risk. Cat scratches can cause permanent damage to an innocent but annoying puppy.

Choose a comfortable, securely fitting collar and leash that is easy for you to work with.

PUPPY KINDERGARTEN

COLLAR AND LEASH

Before you begin your WPG puppy's education, he must be used to his collar and leash. Choose a collar for your puppy that is secure, but not heavy or bulky. He won't enjoy training if he's uncomfortable. A flat buckle collar is fine for everyday wear and for initial puppy training. For older dogs, there are several types of training collars such as the martingale, which is a double loop that tightens slightly around the neck, or the head collar, which is similar to a horse's halter. Do not use a chain choke collar unless you have been specifically shown how to put it on and how to use it. Your breeder will likely suggest other types of training collar more suitable for the WPG.

A lightweight 6-foot woven cotton or nylon training leash is preferred by most trainers because it is easy to fold up in your hand and comfortable to hold because there is a certain amount of give to it. There are lessons where the dog will start off 6 feet away from you at the end of the leash. The leash used to take the puppy outside to relieve himself is shorter because you don't want him to roam away from his area. The shorter leash will also be the one to use when you walk the puppy.

If you've been wise enough to enroll in a puppy kindergarten training class, suggestions will be made as to the best collar and leash for your young puppy. I say "wise" because your puppy will be in a class with puppies in his age range (up to five months old) of all breeds and sizes. It's the perfect way for him to learn the right way (and the wrong way) to interact with other dogs as well as their people. You cannot teach your puppy how to interpret another dog's sign language. For a first-time puppy owner, these socialization classes are invaluable. For experienced dog owners, they are a real boon to further training.

Important life lessons are taught before the puppy even comes home by his first teacher—mom!

ATTENTION

You've been using the dog's name since the minute you collected him from the breeder, so you should be able to get his attention by saying his name—with a big smile and in an excited tone of voice. His response will be the puppy equivalent of "Here I am! What are we going to do?" Your immediate response (if you haven't guessed by now) is "Good dog." Rewarding him at the moment he pays attention to you teaches him the proper way to respond when he hears his name.

BASIC COMMANDS FOR YOUR GRIFF

THE SIT EXERCISE

There are several ways to teach the puppy to sit. The first one is to catch him whenever he is about to sit and, as his backside nears the floor, say "Sit, good dog!" That's positive reinforcement and, if your timing is sharp, he will learn that what he's doing at that

---

SMILE WHEN YOU ORDER ME AROUND!

While trainers recommend practicing with your dog every day, it's perfectly acceptable to take a "mental health day" off. It's better not to train the dog on days when you're in a sour mood. Your bad attitude or lack of interest will be sensed by your dog, and he will respond accordingly. Studies show that dogs are well tuned in to their humans' emotions. Be conscious of how you use your voice when talking to your dog. Raising your voice or shouting will only erode your dog's trust in you as his trainer and master.

An attentive dog is the best student. Choose a distraction-free area for training, and make sure your Griff's attention is focused on the lesson at hand.

second is connected to your saying "Sit" and that you think he's clever for doing it!

Another method is to start with the puppy on his leash in front of you. Show him a treat in the palm of your right hand. Bring your hand up under his nose and, almost in slow motion, move your hand up and back so his nose goes up in the air and his head tilts back as he follows the treat in your hand. At that point, he will have to either sit or fall over, so as his back legs buckle under, say "Sit, good dog," and then give him the treat and lots of praise. You may have to begin with your hand lightly running up his chest, actually lifting his chin up until he sits. Some (usually older) dogs require gentle pressure on their hindquarters with the left hand, in which case the dog should be on your left side. Puppies generally do not appreciate this physical dominance.

After a few times, you should be able to show the dog a treat in the open palm of your hand, raise your hand waist-high as you say "Sit" and have him sit. You thereby will have taught him two things at the same time. Both the verbal command and the motion of the hand are signals for the sit. Your puppy is watching you almost more than he is listening to you, so what you do is just as important as what you say.

Don't save any of these drills only for training sessions. Use them as much as possible at odd times during a normal day. The dog should always sit before being

> **A SIMPLE "SIT"**
> When you command your dog to sit, use the word "Sit." Do not say "Sit down," as your dog will not know whether you mean "Sit" or "Down," or maybe you mean both. Be clear in your instructions to your dog; use one-word commands and always be consistent.

Training

Show your Griff puppy what you mean by "Sit" with some gentle guidance into the correct position.

leash right above his collar in your left hand. Have an extra-special treat, such as a small piece of cooked chicken or hot dog, in your right hand. Place it at the end of the pup's nose and steadily move your hand down and forward along the ground. Hold the leash to prevent a sudden lunge for the food. As the puppy goes into the down position, say "Down" very gently.

The difficulty with this exercise is twofold: it's both the submissive aspect and the fact that most people say the word "Down" as if they were drill sergeants in charge of recruits! So issue the command sweetly, give him the treat and have the pup given his food dish. He should sit to let you go through a doorway first, when the doorbell rings or when you stop to speak to someone on the street.

THE DOWN EXERCISE

Before beginning to teach the down command, you must consider how the dog feels about this exercise. To him, "down" is a submissive position. Being flat on the floor with you standing over him is not his idea of fun. It's up to you to let him know that, while it may not be fun, the reward of your approval is worth his effort.

Start with the puppy on your left side in a sit position. Hold the

The down command can be a challenge.

DOWN

"Down" is a harsh-sounding word and a submissive posture in dog body language, thus presenting two obstacles in teaching the down command. When the dog is about to flop down on his own, tell him "Good down." Pups that are not good about being handled learn better by having food lowered in front of them. A dog that trusts you can be gently guided into position. When you give the command "Down," be sure to say it sweetly!

maintain the down position for several seconds. If he tries to get up immediately, place your hands on his shoulders and press down gently, giving him a very quiet "Good dog." As you progress with this lesson, increase the "down time" until he will hold it until you say "Okay" (his cue for release). Practice this one in the house at various times throughout the day.

By increasing the length of time during which the dog must maintain the down position, you'll find many uses for it. For example, he can lie at your feet in the vet's office or anywhere that both of you have to wait, when you are on the phone, while the family is eating and so forth. If you progress to training for competitive obedience, he'll already be all set for the exercise called the "long down."

"Stay" is a necessary command for your dog's behavior and safety.

THE STAY EXERCISE

You can teach your WPG to stay in the sit, down and stand positions. To teach the sit/stay, have the dog sit on your left side. Hold the leash at waist level in your left hand and let the dog know that you have a treat in your closed right hand. Step forward on your right foot as you say "Stay." Immediately turn and stand directly in front of the dog, keeping your right hand up high so he'll keep his eye on the treat hand and maintain the sit position for a count of five. Return to your original position and offer the reward.

Increase the length of the sit/stay each time until the dog

can hold it for at least 30 seconds without moving. After about a week of success, move out on your right foot and take two steps before turning to face the dog. Give the "Stay" hand signal (left palm up, facing the dog's head) as you leave. He gets the treat when you return and he holds the sit/stay. Increase the distance that you walk away from him before turning until you reach the length of your training leash. But don't rush it! Go back to the beginning if he moves before he should. No matter what the lesson, never be upset by having to back up for a few days. The repetition and practice are what will make your dog reliable in these commands. It won't do any good to move on to something more difficult if the command is not mastered at the easier levels. Above all, even if you do get frustrated, never let your puppy know. Always keep a positive, upbeat attitude during training, which will transmit to your dog for positive results.

The down/stay is taught in the same way once the dog is completely reliable and steady with the down command. Again, don't rush it. With the dog in the down position on your left side, step out on your right foot as you say "Stay." Return by walking around in back of the dog and into your original position. While you are training, it's okay to murmur something like "Hold on" to encourage him to stay put. When the dog will stay without moving when you are at a distance of 3 or 4 feet, begin to increase the length of time before you return. Be sure he holds the down on your return until you say "Okay." At that point, he gets his treat—just so he'll remember for next time that it's not over until it's over.

THE COME EXERCISE

No command is more important to the safety of your WPG than "Come." It is what you should say every single time you see the puppy running toward you: "Rupert, come! Good dog." During playtime, run a few feet away

If your puppy likes to follow you everywhere you go, use this to your advantage in training. It is a good head start for both the come command and heel-training.

You want your Griff to come to you enthusiastically when he hears your call.

from the puppy and turn and tell him to "Come" as he is already running to you. You can go so far as to teach your puppy two things at once if you squat down and hold out your arms. As the pup gets close to you and you're saying "Good dog," bring your right arm in about waist high. Now he's also learning the hand signal, an excellent device should you be on the phone when you need to get him to come to you. You'll also both be one step ahead when you enter obedience classes.

When the puppy responds to your well-timed "Come," try it with the puppy on the training leash. This time, catch him off guard, while he's sniffing a leaf or watching a bird: "Rupert, come!" You may have to pause for a split second after his name to be sure you have his attention. If the puppy shows any sign of confusion, give the leash a mild jerk and take a couple of steps backward. Do not repeat the command. In this case, you should say "Good come" as he reaches you.

That's the number-one rule of training. Each command word is given just once. Anything more is nagging. You'll also notice that all commands are one word only. Even when they are actually two words, you say them as one.

Never call the dog to come to you—with or without his name—if you are angry or intend to correct him for some misbehavior. When correcting the pup, you go to him. Your dog must always connect "Come" with something pleasant and with your approval; then you can rely on his response.

Puppies, like children, have notoriously short attention spans, so don't overdo it with any of the training. Keep each lesson short. Break it up with a quick run

LET'S GO!
Many people use "Let's go" instead of "Heel" when teaching their dogs to behave on lead. It sounds more like fun! When beginning to teach the heel, whatever command you use, always step off on your left foot. That's the one next to the dog, who is on your left side, in case you've forgotten. Keep a loose leash. When the dog pulls ahead, stop, bring him back and begin again. Use treats to guide him around turns.

around the yard or a ball toss, repeat the lesson and quit as soon as the pup gets it right. That way, you will always end with a "Good dog."

Life isn't perfect and neither are puppies. A time will come, often around 10 months of age, when he'll become "selectively deaf" or choose to "forget" his name. He may respond by wagging his tail (and even seeming to smile at you) with a look that says "Make me!" Laugh, throw his favorite toy and skip the lesson you had planned. Pups will be pups!

THE HEEL EXERCISE

The second most important command to teach, after the come, is the heel. When you are walking your growing puppy, you need to be in control. Besides, it looks terrible to be pulled and yanked down the street, and it's not much fun either. Your eight- to ten-week-old puppy will probably follow you everywhere, but that's his natural instinct, not your control over the situation. However, any time he does follow you, you can say "Heel" and be ahead of the game, as he will learn to associate this command with the action of following you before you even begin teaching him to heel.

There is a very precise, almost military, procedure for teaching your dog to heel. As with all other obedience training, begin with the dog on your left side. He will be in a very nice sit and you will have the training leash across your chest. Hold the loop and folded leash in your right hand. Pick up the slack leash above the dog in your left hand and hold it loosely at your side. Step out on your left foot as you say "Heel." If the puppy does not move, give a gentle tug or pat your left leg to get him started. If he surges ahead of you, stop and pull him back gently until he is at your side. Tell him to sit and begin again.

Proper leash behavior is important to teach early on, before you have an adult WPG taking you for walks.

The heel exercise must be mastered by show and pet dogs alike. A show dog must heel at the handler's side while the judge evaluates the dog's gait.

Walk a few steps and stop while the puppy is correctly beside you. Tell him to sit and give mild verbal praise. (More enthusiastic praise will encourage him to think the lesson is over.) Repeat the lesson, increasing the number of steps you take only as long as the dog is heeling nicely beside you. When you end the lesson, have him hold the sit, then give him the "Okay" to let him know that this is the end of the lesson. Praise him so that he knows he did a good job.

The cure for excessive pulling (a common problem) is to stop when the dog is no more than 2 or 3 feet ahead of you. Guide him back into position and begin again. With a really determined puller, try switching to a head collar. When used properly, this will automatically turn the pup's head toward you so you can bring him back easily to the heel position. Give quiet, reassuring praise every time the leash goes slack and he's staying with you.

Staying and heeling can take a lot out of a dog, so provide playtime and free-running exercise to shake off the stress when the lessons are over. You don't want him to associate training with all work and no fun.

Training 103

The hunter attaches a bell to the Griff's collar to help keep track of the dog. While the dog is moving in the field, the bell rings, but when the dog freezes on point, the bell stops. This is the hunter's signal to go to his dog and flush and kill the game.

Participating in activities with your WPG is a great way to further your bond with your canine best friend, and there is so much that he is capable of.

OBEDIENCE CLASSES

The advantages of an obedience class are that your dog will have to learn amid the distractions of other people and dogs and that your mistakes will be quickly corrected by the trainer. Teaching your dog along with a qualified instructor and other handlers who may have more dog experience than you is another plus of the class environment. The instructor and other handlers can help you find the most efficient way of teaching your dog a command or exercise. It's often easier to learn from other people's mistakes than from your own. You will also learn all of the requirements for competitive obedience trials, in which you can earn titles and go on to advanced jumping and retrieving exercises, which are fun for many dogs. Obedience classes build the foundation needed for many other canine activities (in which we humans are allowed to participate, too).

BEYOND OBEDIENCE

Basic obedience is critical to every dog, whether he's a show dog, hunting dog and/or pet dog, but these lessons will not make up your Griffon's whole repertory. For the hunting dog, there are some basic lessons that you will need to initiate. Fortunately in the WPG you have a genius of a hunting breed—the "supreme gundog," as the AKC standard aptly describes—and not too much specific training is required to get the dog on his feet in the field. The WPG instinctively learns the ins and outs of hunting, and the owner doesn't have to do too much in the way of formal training.

The first year of the Griffon's education and in-the-field experience is absolutely critical. The owner must expose the puppy to hunting situations early on. Some great dogs have been ruined by their owners' failure to expose the dogs to the field until after they were a year old. The dog's love of the hunt will burn through in no time at all. You will see it click in your dog's face and growing body—especially the moment his little body freezes in its first point, which can happen at quite a young age. Keep the hunt fun and lively, and don't expect the WPG puppy to perform like a seasoned Field Champion in the first month. His talents will blossom sooner than you think, though some dogs do take longer to catch on.

Work on the come (or "here") command with the puppy: this exercise is do or die in the field. The come and the "whoa" commands give the hunter control of his dog when they are working. Griffs instinctively work close to their masters in the field, which is a plus for the hunter to have a dog that pays attention to his commands naturally. As the puppy grows, you will expose the puppy to water and dead birds, then birds in cover, gunfire and so on. The assistance of an experienced hunter will pay off more than any chapter in a book. Certainly there are some excellent introductory hunting books available to assist the WPG owner in training the puppy, though the best education will come directly from the Griff himself. This versatile hunter can do it all—hunt, point and retrieve, and you will marvel at the God-given abilities of your WPG. Highly intelligent and instinctual, the WPG can be a challenge to train at the highest levels of field performance. Experienced, dedicated owners excel with these dogs, though they are too much for the novice or casual hunter to handle.

For a dog whose traditional use is hunting in the field, his reliable response to the hunter's commands is essential.

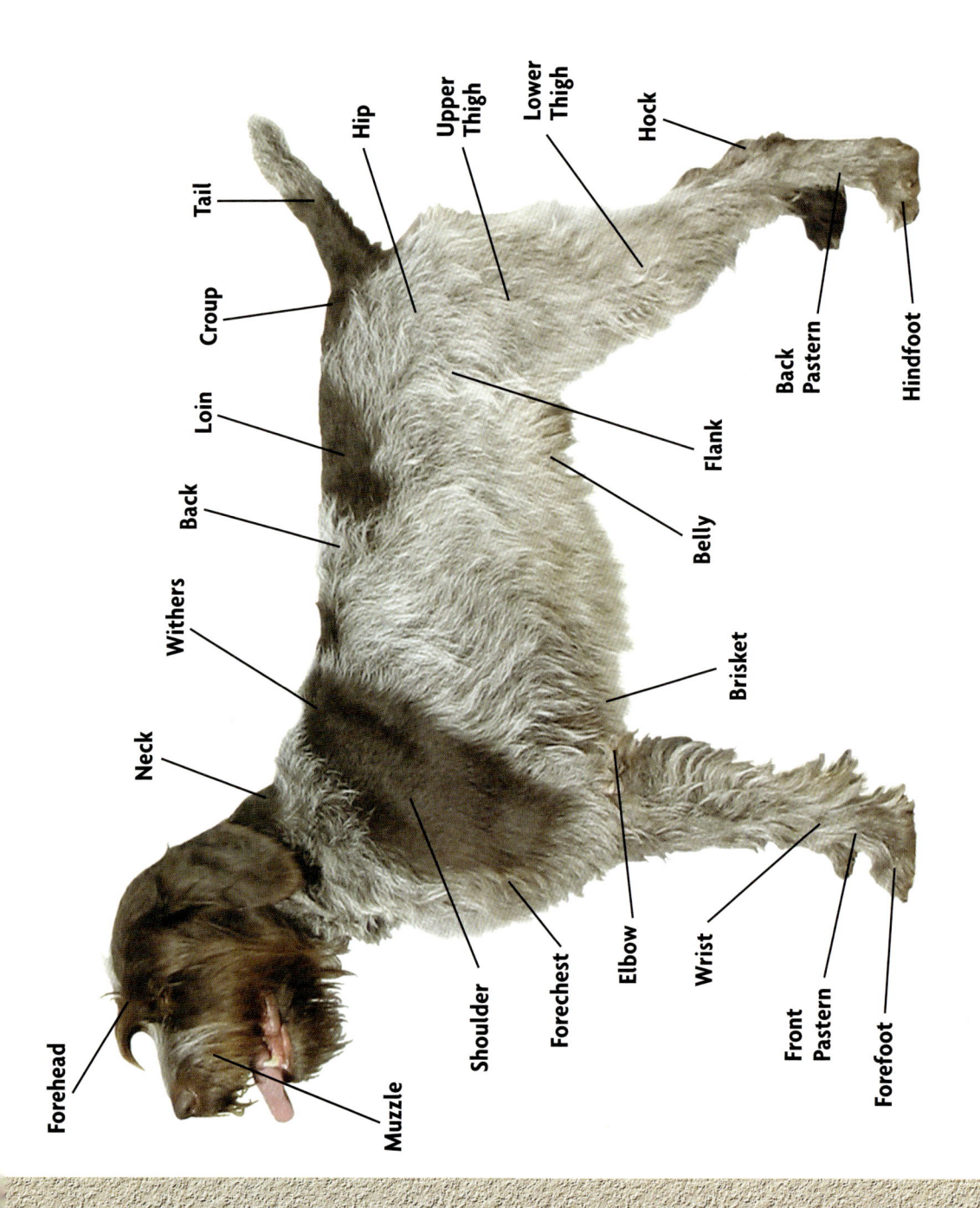

Physical Structure of the Wirehaired Pointing Griffon

HEALTHCARE OF YOUR

WIREHAIRED POINTING GRIFFON

By Lowell Ackerman, DVM, DACVD

HEALTHCARE FOR A LIFETIME
When you own a dog, you become his healthcare advocate over his entire lifespan, as well as being the one to shoulder the financial burden of such care. Accordingly, it is worthwhile to focus on prevention rather than treatment, as you and your pet will both be happier.

Of course, the best place to have begun your program of preventive healthcare is with the initial purchase or adoption of your dog. There is no way of guaranteeing that your new furry friend is free of medical problems, but there are some things you can do to improve your odds. You certainly should have done adequate research into the WPG and have selected your puppy carefully rather than buying on impulse. Health issues aside, a large number of pet abandonment and relinquishment cases arise from a mismatch between pet needs and owner expectations. This is entirely preventable with appropriate planning and finding a good breeder.

Regarding healthcare issues specifically, it is very difficult to make blanket statements about where to acquire a problem-free pet, but, again, a reputable breeder is your best bet. In an ideal situation you have the opportunity to see both parents, get references from other owners of the breeder's pups and see genetic-testing documentation for several generations of the litter's ancestors. At the very least, you must thoroughly investigate the Wirehaired Pointing Griffon and the problems inherent in that breed, as well as the genetic testing available to screen for those problems. Genetic testing offers some important benefits, but testing is available for only a few disorders in a relatively small number of breeds and is not available for some of the most common genetic diseases, such as hip dysplasia, cataracts, epilepsy, cardiomyopathy, etc. This area of research is indeed exciting and increasingly important, and advances will continue to be made each year. In fact, recent research has shown that there is an equivalent dog gene for 75% of known human genes, so research done in either species is likely to benefit the other.

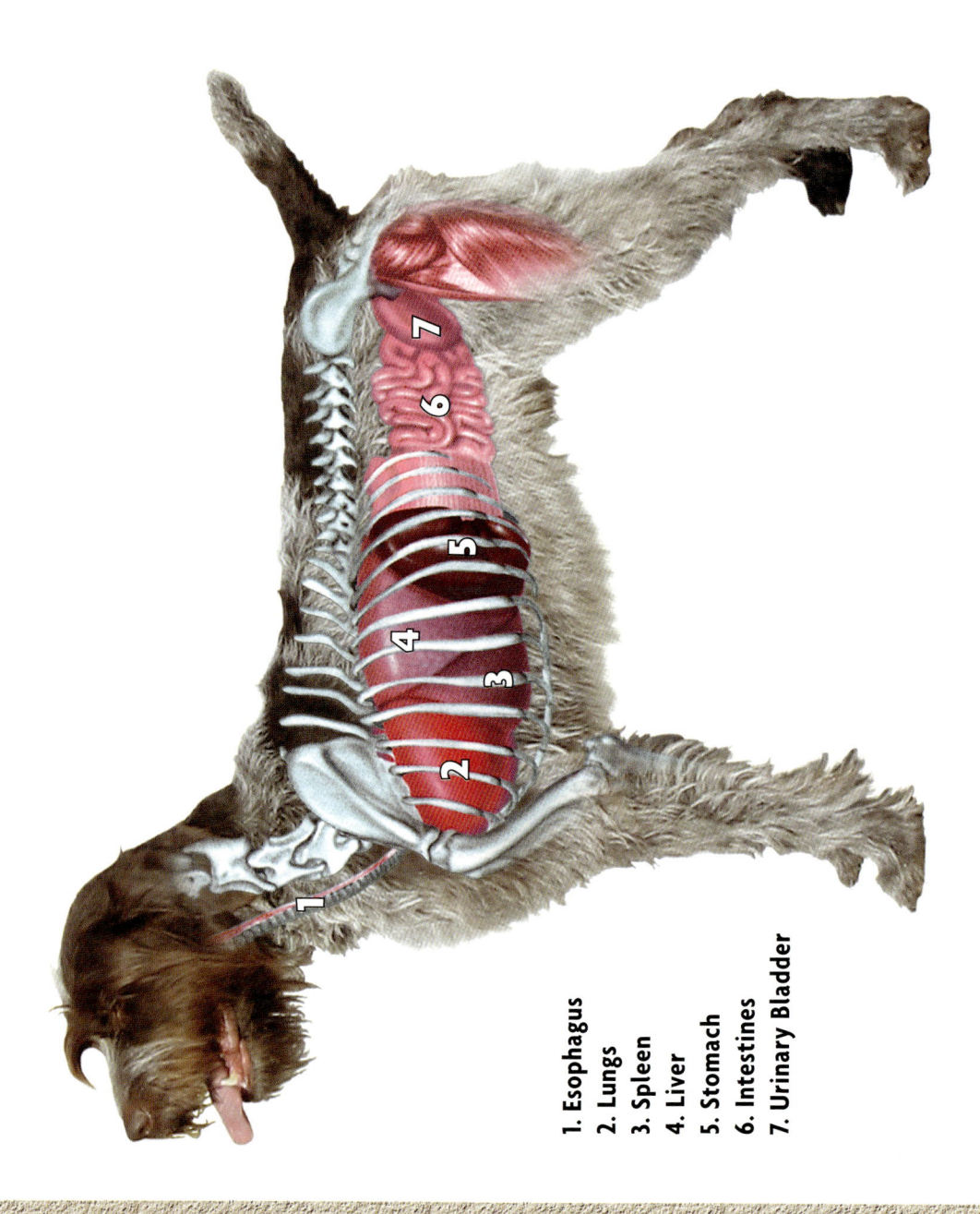

1. Esophagus
2. Lungs
3. Spleen
4. Liver
5. Stomach
6. Intestines
7. Urinary Bladder

INTERNAL ORGANS OF THE WIREHAIRED POINTING GRIFFON

We've also discussed that evaluating the behavioral nature of your WPG and that of his immediate family members is an important part of the selection process that cannot be underestimated or overemphasized. It is sometimes difficult to evaluate temperament in puppies because certain behavioral tendencies, such as some forms of aggression, may not be immediately evident. More dogs are euthanized each year for behavioral reasons than for all medical conditions combined, so it is critical to take temperament issues seriously. Start with a well-balanced, friendly companion and put the time and effort into proper socialization, and you will both be rewarded with a lifelong valued relationship.

Assuming that you have started off with a pup from healthy, sound stock, you then become responsible for helping your veterinarian keep your pet healthy. Some crucial things happen before you even bring your puppy home. Parasite control typically begins at two weeks of age, and vaccinations typically begin at six to eight weeks of age. A pre-pubertal evaluation is typically scheduled for about six months of age. At this time, a dental evaluation is done (since the adult teeth are now in), heartworm prevention is started and neutering or spaying is most commonly done.

It is critical to commence regular dental care at home if you have not already done so. It may not sound very important, but most dogs have active periodontal disease by four years of age if they don't have their teeth cleaned regularly at home, not just at their veterinary exams. Dental problems lead to more than just bad "doggy breath." Gum disease can have very serious medical consequences. If you start brushing your dog's teeth and using antiseptic rinses from a young age, your dog will be accustomed to it and will not resist. The results will be healthy dentition, which your pet will need to enjoy a long, healthy life.

Most dogs are considered adults at a year of age, although some larger breeds still have some filling out to do up to about two or so years old. Even individual dogs within each breed have different healthcare requirements, so work with your veterinarian to determine what will be needed and what your role should be. This doctor-client relationship is important, because as vaccination guidelines change, there may not be an annual "vaccine visit" scheduled. You must make sure that you see your veterinarian at least annually, even if no vaccines are due, because this is the best opportunity to coordinate healthcare activities and to make sure

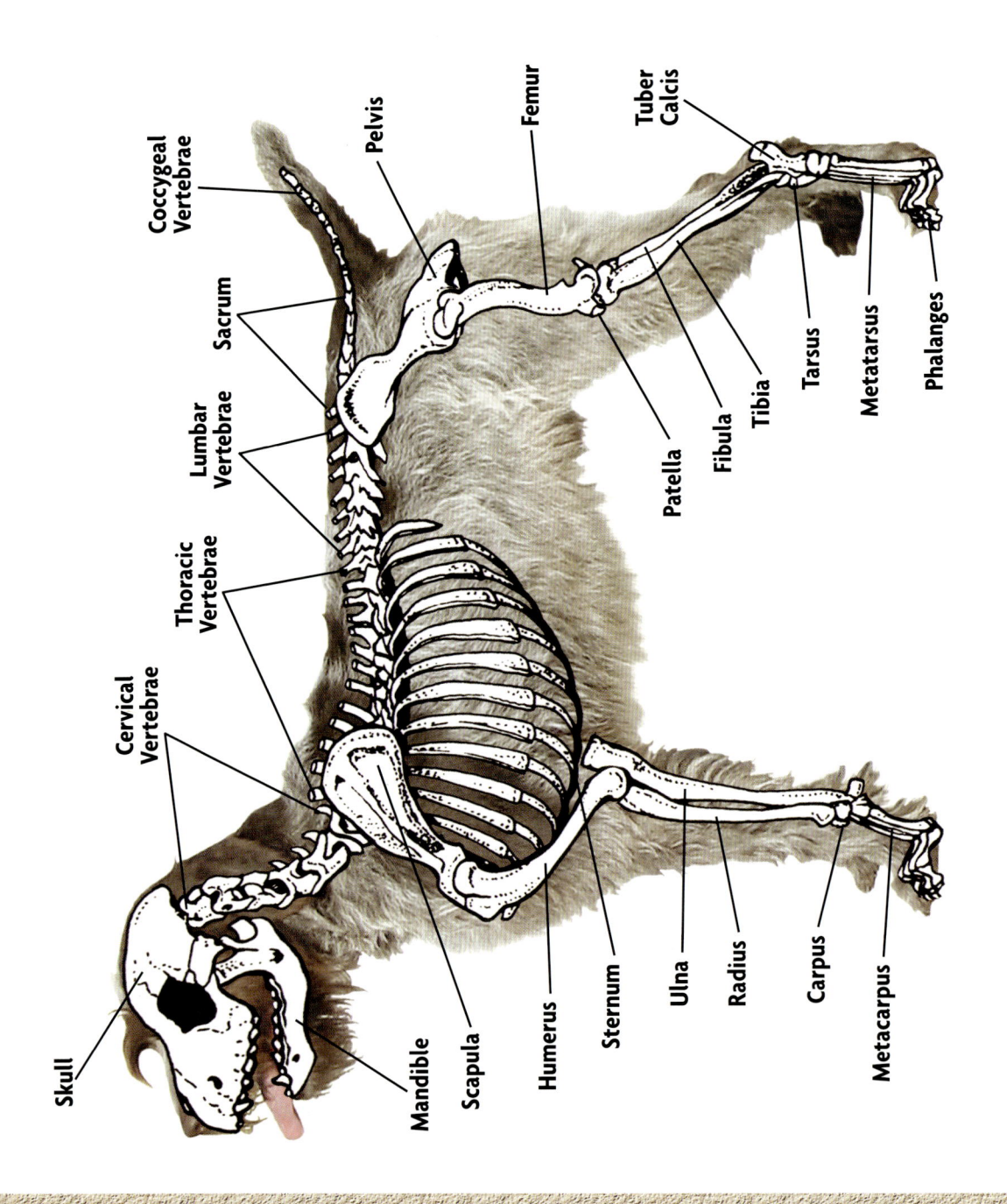

Skeletal Structure of the Wirehaired Pointing Griffon

Healthcare

that no medical issues creep by unaddressed.

When your WPG reaches three-quarters of his anticipated lifespan, he is considered a "senior" and likely requires some special care. In general, if you've been taking great care of your canine companion throughout his formative and adult years, the transition to senior status should be a smooth one. Age is not a disease, and as long as everything is functioning as it should, there is no reason why most of late adulthood should not be rewarding for both you and your pet. This is especially true if you have tended to the details, such as regular veterinary visits, proper dental care, excellent nutrition and management of bone and joint issues.

At this stage in your WPG's life, your veterinarian may want to schedule visits twice yearly, instead of once, to run some laboratory screenings, electrocardiograms and the like, and to change the diet to something more digestible. Catching problems early is the best way to manage them effectively. Treating the early stages of heart disease is so much easier than trying to intervene when there is more significant damage to the heart muscle. Similarly, managing the beginning of kidney problems is fairly routine if there is no significant kidney damage. Other problems,

> **DENTAL WARNING SIGNS**
> A veterinary dental exam is necessary if you notice one or any combination of the following in your dog:
> - Broken, loose or missing teeth
> - Loss of appetite (which could be due to mouth pain or illness caused by infection)
> - Gum abnormalities, including redness, swelling and bleeding
> - Drooling, with or without blood
> - Yellowing of the teeth or gumline, indicating tartar
> - Bad breath

like cognitive dysfunction (similar to senility and Alzheimer's disease), cancer, diabetes and arthritis, are more common in older dogs, but all can be treated to help the dog live as many happy, comfortable years as possible. Just as in people, medical management is more effective (and less expensive) when you catch things early.

SELECTING A VETERINARIAN

There is probably no more important decision that you will make regarding your pet's healthcare than the selection of his doctor. Your pet's veterinarian will be a pediatrician, family-practice physician and gerontologist, depending on the dog's life stage, and will be the individual who makes recommendations regarding issues such as when

After time outdoors, check your WPG's feet to make sure nothing has become embedded in the pads that could cause the dog discomfort.

specialists need to be consulted, when diagnostic testing and/or therapeutic intervention is needed and when you will need to seek outside emergency and critical-care services. Your vet will act as your advocate and liaison throughout these processes.

Everyone has his own idea about what to look for in a vet, an individual who will play a big role in his dog's (and, of course, his own) life for many years to come. For some, it is the compassionate caregiver with whom they hope to develop a professional relationship to span the lives of their dogs and even their future pets. For others, they are seeking a clinician with keen diagnostic and therapeutic insight who can deliver state-of-the-art healthcare. Still others need a veterinary facility that is open evenings and weekends, is in close proximity or provides mobile veterinary services to accommodate their schedules; these people may not much mind that their dogs might see different veterinarians on each visit. Just as we have different reasons for selecting our own healthcare professionals (e.g., covered by insurance plan, expert in field, convenient location, etc.), we should not expect that there is a one-size-fits-all recommendation for selecting a veterinarian and veterinary practice. The best advice is to be honest in your assessment of what you expect from a veterinary practice and to conscientiously research the options in your area. You will quickly appreciate that not all veterinary practices are the same, and you will be happiest with one that truly meets your needs.

There is another point to be considered in the selection of veterinary services. Not that long ago, a single veterinarian would attempt to manage all medical and surgical issues as they arose. That was often problematic, because veterinarians are trained in many species and many diseases, and it was just impossible for general veterinary practitioners to be experts in every species, every breed, every field and every ailment. However, just as in the human healthcare fields, specialization has allowed general practitioners to concentrate on primary healthcare delivery, especially wellness and the prevention of infectious diseases, and to utilize a network of specialists to assist in the management of conditions that require specific expertise and experience. Thus there are now many types of veterinary specialists, including dermatologists, cardiologists, ophthalmologists, surgeons, internists, oncologists, neurologists, behaviorists, criticalists and others to help primary-care veterinarians deal with complicated medical challenges. In most cases, specialists see cases referred by primary-care veterinarians, make diagnoses and set up management plans. From there, the animals' ongoing care is returned to their primary-care veterinarians. This important team approach to your pet's medical-care needs has provided opportunities for advanced care and an unparalleled level of quality to be delivered.

With all of the opportunities for your WPG to receive high-quality veterinary medical care, there is another topic that needs to be addressed at the same time—cost. It's been said that you can have excellent healthcare or inexpensive healthcare, but never both; this is as true in veterinary medicine as it is in human medicine. While veterinary costs are a fraction of what the same services cost in the human healthcare arena, it is still difficult to deal with unanticipated medical costs, especially since they can easily creep into hundreds or even thousands of dollars if specialists or emergency services become involved. However, there are ways of managing these risks. The easiest is to buy pet health insurance and realize that its foremost purpose is not to cover routine healthcare visits but rather to serve as an umbrella for those

Like people, dogs can develop skin problems from grass, flowers and/or airborne allergies. Consult your vet if skin and coat problems persist.

Common Infectious Diseases

Let's discuss some of the diseases that create the need for vaccination in the first place. Following are the major canine infectious diseases and a simple explanation of each.

Rabies: A devastating viral disease that can be fatal in dogs and people. In fact, vaccination of dogs and cats is an important public-health measure to create a resistant animal buffer population to protect people from contracting the disease. Vaccination schedules are determined on a government level and are not optional for pet owners; rabies vaccination is required by law in all 50 states.

Parvovirus: A severe, potentially life-threatening disease that is easily transmitted between dogs. There are four strains of the virus, but it is believed that there is significant "cross-protection" between strains that may be included in individual vaccines.

Distemper: A potentially severe and life-threatening disease with a relatively high risk of exposure, especially in certain regions. In very high-risk distemper environments, young pups may be vaccinated with human measles vaccine, a related virus that offers cross-protection when administered at four to ten weeks of age.

Hepatitis: Caused by canine adenovirus type 1 (CAV-1), but since vaccination with the causative virus has a higher rate of adverse effects, cross-protection is derived from the use of adenovirus type 2 (CAV-2), a cause of respiratory disease and one of the potential causes of canine cough. Vaccination with CAV-2 provides long-term immunity against hepatitis, but relatively less protection against respiratory infection.

Canine cough: Also called tracheobronchitis, actually a fairly complicated result of viral and bacterial offenders; therefore, even with vaccination, protection is incomplete. Wherever dogs congregate, canine cough will likely be spread among them. Intranasal vaccination with *Bordetella* and parainfluenza is the best safeguard, but the duration of immunity does not appear to be very long, typically a year at most. These are non-core vaccines, but vaccination is sometimes mandated by boarding kennels, obedience classes, dog shows and other places where dogs congregate to try to minimize spread of infection.

Leptospirosis: A potentially fatal disease that is more common in some geographic regions. It is capable of being spread to humans. The disease varies with the individual "serovar," or strain, of *Leptospira* involved. Since there does not appear to be much cross-protection between serovars, protection is only as good as the likelihood that the serovar in the vaccine is the same as the one in the pet's local environment. Problems with *Leptospira* vaccines are that protection does not last very long, side effects are not uncommon and a large percentage of dogs (perhaps 30%) may not respond to vaccination.

Borrelia burgdorferi: The cause of Lyme disease, the risk of which varies with the geographic area in which the pet lives and travels. Lyme disease is spread by deer ticks in the eastern US and western black-legged ticks in the western part of the country, and the risk of exposure is high in some regions. Lameness, fever and inappetence are most commonly seen in affected dogs. The extent of protection from the vaccine has not been conclusively demonstrated.

Coronavirus: This disease has a high risk of exposure, especially in areas where dogs congregate, but it typically causes only mild to moderate digestive upset (diarrhea, vomiting, etc.). Vaccines are available, but the duration of protection is believed to be relatively short and the effectiveness of the vaccine in preventing infection is considered low.

There are many other vaccinations available, including those for *Giardia* and canine adenovirus-1. While there may be some specific indications for their use, and local risk factors to be considered, they are not widely recommended for most dogs.

rainy days when your pet needs medical care and you don't want to worry about whether or not you can afford that care.

Pet insurance policies are very cost-effective (and very inexpensive by human health-insurance standards), but make sure that you buy the policy long before you intend to use it (preferably starting in puppyhood, because coverage will exclude pre-existing conditions) and that you are actually buying an indemnity insurance plan from an insurance company that is regulated by your state or province. Many insurance policy look-alikes are actually discount clubs that are redeemable only at specific locations and for specific services. An indemnity plan covers your pet at almost all veterinary, specialty and emergency practices and is an excellent way to manage your pet's ongoing healthcare needs.

VACCINATIONS AND INFECTIOUS DISEASES

There has never been an easier time to prevent a variety of infectious diseases in your dog, but the advances we've made in veterinary medicine come with a price—choice. Now while it may seem that choice is a good thing (and it is), it has never been more difficult for the pet owner (or the veterinarian) to make an informed decision about the best way to protect pets through vaccination.

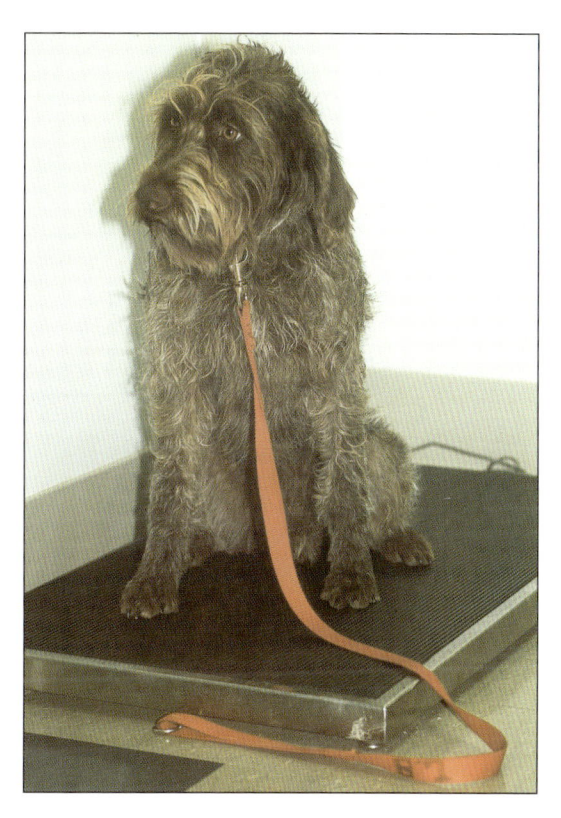

Years ago, it was just accepted that puppies got a starter series of vaccinations and then annual "boosters" throughout their lives to keep them protected. As more and more vaccines became available, consumers wanted the convenience of having all of that protection in a single injection. The result was "multivalent" vaccines that crammed a lot of protection into a single syringe. The manufacturers' recommendations were to give the vaccines annually, and this was a simple enough protocol to follow.

How does your Griff weigh in? A healthy weight is important for good overall health.

Ready for action! Maintaining a healthy, alert dog depends largely on the selection of a qualified veterinarian.

However, as veterinary medicine has become more sophisticated and we have started looking more at healthcare quandaries rather than convenience, it became necessary to reevaluate the situation and deal with some tough questions. It is important to realize that whether or not to use a particular vaccine depends on the risk of contracting the disease against which it protects, the severity of the disease if it is contracted, the duration of immunity provided by the vaccine, the safety of the product and the needs of the individual animal. In a very general sense, rabies, distemper, hepatitis and parvovirus are considered core vaccine needs, while parainfluenza, *Bordetella bronchiseptica*, leptospirosis, coronavirus and borreliosis (Lyme disease) are considered non-core needs and best reserved for animals that demonstrate reasonable risk of contracting the diseases.

NEUTERING/SPAYING

Sterilization procedures (neutering for males/spaying for females) are meant to accomplish several purposes. While the underlying premise is to address the risk of pet overpopulation, there are also some medical and behavioral benefits to the surgeries as well. For females, spaying may lead to a marked reduction in the risk of mammary cancer. There also will be no manifestations of "heat" to attract male dogs and no bleeding in the house. For males, there is prevention of testicular cancer and a reduction in the risk of prostate problems. In both sexes there may be some limited reduction in aggressive behaviors toward other dogs, and some diminishing of urine marking, roaming and mounting.

While neutering and spaying do indeed prevent animals from contributing to pet overpopulation, even no-cost and low-cost neutering options have not eliminated the problem. Perhaps one of the main reasons for this

Healthcare

is that individuals that intentionally breed their dogs and those that allow their animals to run at large are the main causes of unwanted offspring. Also, animals in shelters are often there because they were abandoned or relinquished, not because they came from unplanned matings. Neutering/spaying is important, but it should be considered in the context of the real causes of animals' ending up in shelters and eventually being euthanized.

One of the important considerations regarding neutering is that it is a surgical procedure. This sometimes gets lost in discussions of low-cost procedures and commoditization of the process. In females, spaying is specifically referred to as an ovariohysterectomy. In this procedure, a midline incision is made in the abdomen and the entire uterus and both ovaries are surgically removed. While this is a major invasive surgical procedure, it usually has few complications, because it is typically performed on healthy young animals. However, it is major surgery, as any woman who has had a hysterectomy will attest.

In males, neutering has traditionally referred to castration, which involves the surgical removal of both testicles. While still a significant piece of surgery, there is not the abdominal exposure that is required in the female surgery. In addition, there is now a chemical sterilization option, in which a solution is injected into each testicle, leading to atrophy of the sperm-producing cells. This can typically be done under sedation rather than full anesthesia. This is a relatively new approach, and there are no long-term clinical studies yet available.

When to neuter/spay a dog continues to be a much-debated question. Veterinarians and breeders have different theories, each informed by varying goals and philosophies. Most veterinarians encourage pet owners to neuter/spay their dogs at around six months, citing health advantages to early surgeries. Many dog breeders consider six months too early, including most WPG breeders. Large breeds and hunting dogs benefit from postponing neutering/spaying until the dog or bitch is one year of age. The extra six months allows hormonal advantages for the dog's proper growth and physical development. This is especially important with male dogs that may not achieve their full size, skull proportion and chest depth if neutered before a year. Some breeders recommend waiting until the dog is two years of age. Each owner should discuss the matter with his veterinarian and breeder to decide what's best for his dog.

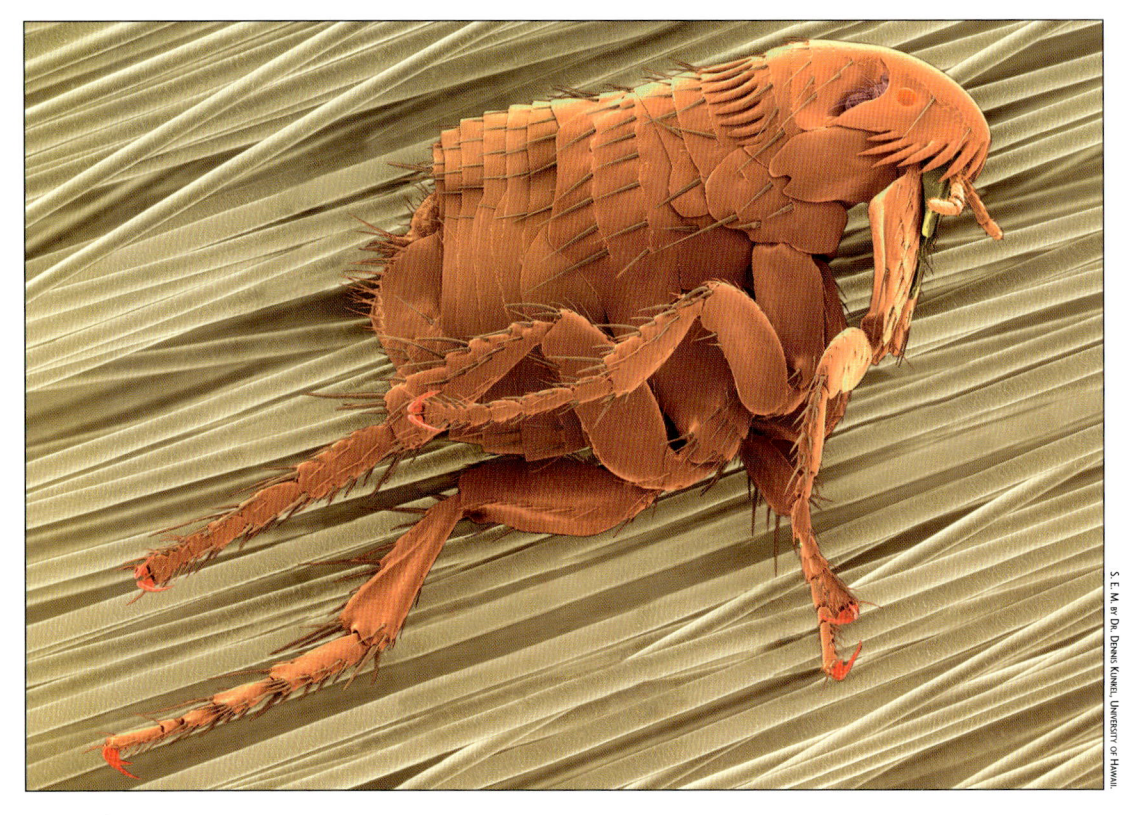

A scanning electron micrograph of a dog flea, *Ctenocephalides canis*, on dog hair.

EXTERNAL PARASITES

FLEAS

Fleas have been around for millions of years and, while we have better tools now for controlling them than at any time in the past, there still is little chance that they will end up on an endangered species list. Actually, they are very well adapted to living on our pets, and they continue to adapt as we make advances.

The female flea can consume 15 times her weight in blood during active reproduction and can lay as many as 40 eggs a day. These eggs are very resistant to the effects of insecticides. They hatch into larvae, which then mature and spin cocoons. The immature fleas reside in this pupal stage until the time is right for feeding. This pupal stage is also very resistant to the effects of insecticides, and pupae can last in the environment without feeding for many months. Newly emergent fleas are attracted to animals by the warmth of the animals' bodies, movement and exhaled carbon dioxide. However, when they first emerge from their cocoons, they orient towards light; thus when an animal passes between a flea and the light source, casting a shadow, the flea pounces and starts to feed. If the animal turns out to be a dog or cat, the reproductive cycle continues. If the flea lands on another type of animal, including a person, the flea will bite but will then look for a more appropriate host. An emerging adult flea can survive without feeding for up to 12 months but, once it tastes blood, it can survive off its host for only 3 to 4 days.

It was once thought that fleas spend most of their lives in the environment, but we now know that fleas won't willingly jump off a dog unless leaping to another dog or when physically removed by brushing, bathing or other manipulation. Flea eggs, on the other hand, are shiny and smooth, and they roll off the animal and into the environment. The eggs, larvae and pupae then exist in the environment, but once the adult finds a susceptible animal, it's home sweet home until the flea is forced to seek refuge elsewhere.

Since adult fleas live on the animal and immature forms survive in the environment, a successful treatment plan must address all stages of the flea life cycle. There are now several safe and effective flea-control products that can be applied on a monthly basis. These include fipronil, imidacloprid, selamectin and permethrin (found in several formulations). Most of these products have significant flea-killing rates within 24 hours. However, none of them will control the immature forms in the environment. To accomplish this, there are a variety of insect growth regulators that can be

FLEA PREVENTION FOR YOUR DOG

- Discuss with your veterinarian the safest product to protect your dog, likely in the form of a monthly tablet or a liquid preparation placed on the back of the dog's neck.
- For dogs suffering from flea-bite dermatitis, a shampoo or topical insecticide treatment is required.
- Your lawn and property should be sprayed with an insecticide designed to kill fleas and ticks that lurk outdoors.
- Using a flea comb, check the dog's coat regularly for any signs of parasites.
- Practice good housekeeping. Vacuum floors, carpets and furniture regularly, especially in the areas that the dog frequents, and wash the dog's bedding weekly.
- Follow up house-cleaning with carpet shampoos and sprays to rid the house of fleas at all stages of development. Insect growth regulators are the safest option.

THE FLEA'S LIFE CYCLE

What came first, the flea or the egg? This age-old mystery is more difficult to comprehend than the actual cycle of the flea. Fleas usually live only about four months. A female can lay 2,000 eggs in her lifetime.

Egg

After ten days of rolling around your carpet or under your furniture, the eggs hatch into larvae, which feed on various and sundry debris. In days or months, depending on the climate, the larvae spin cocoons and develop into the pupal or nymph stage, which quickly develop into fleas.

Larva

Pupa

These immature fleas must locate a host within 10 to 14 days or they will die. Only about 1% of the flea population exist as adult fleas, while the other 99% exist as eggs, larvae or pupae.

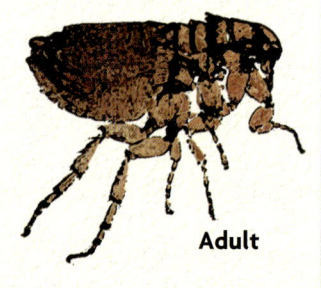

Adult

KILL FLEAS THE NATURAL WAY

If you choose not to go the route of conventional medication, there are some natural ways to ward off fleas:

- Dust your dog with a natural flea powder, composed of such herbal goodies as rosemary, wormwood, pennyroyal, citronella, rue, tobacco powder and eucalyptus.
- Apply diatomaceous earth, the fossilized remains of single-cell algae, to your carpets, furniture and pet's bedding. Even though it's not good for dogs, it's even worse for fleas, which will dry up swiftly and die.
- Brush your dog frequently, give him adequate exercise and let him fast occasionally. All of these activities strengthen the dog's immune system and make him more resistant to disease and parasites.
- Bathe your dog with a capful of pennyroyal or eucalyptus oil.
- Feed a natural diet, free of additives and preservatives. Add some fresh garlic and brewer's yeast to the dog's morning portion, as these items have flea-repelling properties.

sprayed into the environment (e.g., pyriproxyfen, methoprene, fenoxycarb) as well as insect development inhibitors such as lufenuron that can be administered. These compounds have no effect on adult fleas, but they stop immature forms from developing into adults. In years gone by, we relied heavily on toxic insecticides (such as organophosphates, organochlorines and carbamates) to manage the flea problem, but today's options are not only much safer to use on our pets but also safer for the environment.

TICKS

Ticks are members of the spider class (arachnids) and are bloodsucking parasites capable of transmitting a variety of diseases, including Lyme disease, ehrlichiosis, babesiosis and Rocky Mountain spotted fever. It's easy to see ticks on your own skin, but it is more of a challenge when your furry companion is affected. Whenever you happen to be planning a stroll in a tick-infested area (especially forests, grassy or wooded areas or parks) be prepared to do a thorough inspection of your dog afterward to search for ticks. Ticks can be tricky, so make sure you spend time looking in the ears, between the toes and everywhere else where a tick might hide. Ticks need to be attached for 24–72 hours before they transmit most of the diseases that they carry, so you do have a window of opportunity for some preventive intervention.

A TICKING BOMB
There is nothing good about a tick's harpooning his nose into your dog's skin. Among the diseases caused by ticks are Rocky Mountain spotted fever, canine ehrlichiosis, canine babesiosis, canine hepatozoonosis and Lyme disease. If a dog is allergic to the saliva of a female wood tick, he can develop tick paralysis.

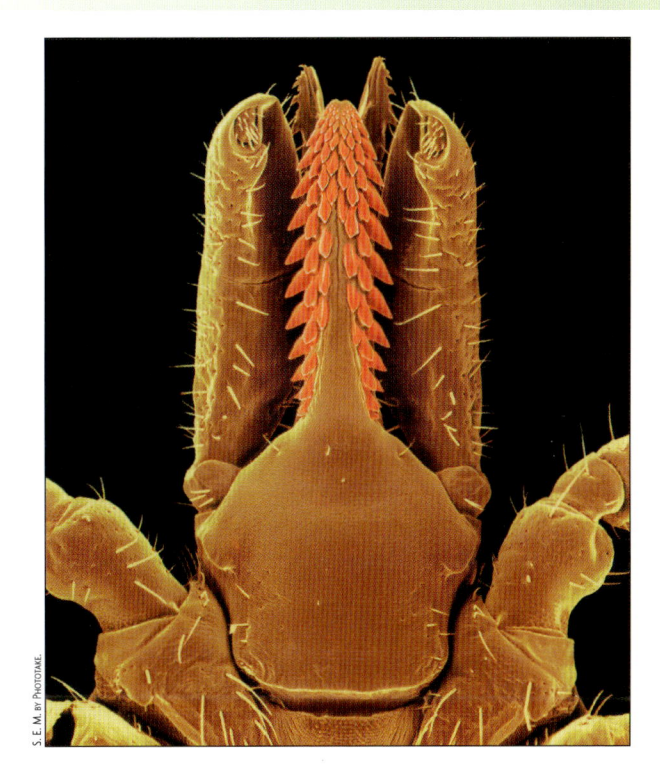

Female ticks live to eat and breed. They can lay between 4,000 and 5,000 eggs and they die soon after. Males, on the other hand, live only to mate with the females and continue the process as long as they are able. Most ticks live on multiple hosts before parasitizing dogs. The immature forms typically reside on grass and shrubs, waiting for susceptible animals to walk by. The larvae and nymph stages typically feed on wildlife.

If only a few ticks are present on a dog, they can be plucked out, but it is important to remove the entire head and mouthparts,

A scanning electron micrograph of the head of a female deer tick, *Ixodes dammini*, a parasitic tick that carries Lyme disease.

WIREHAIRED POINTING GRIFFON

Deer tick, Ixodes dammini.

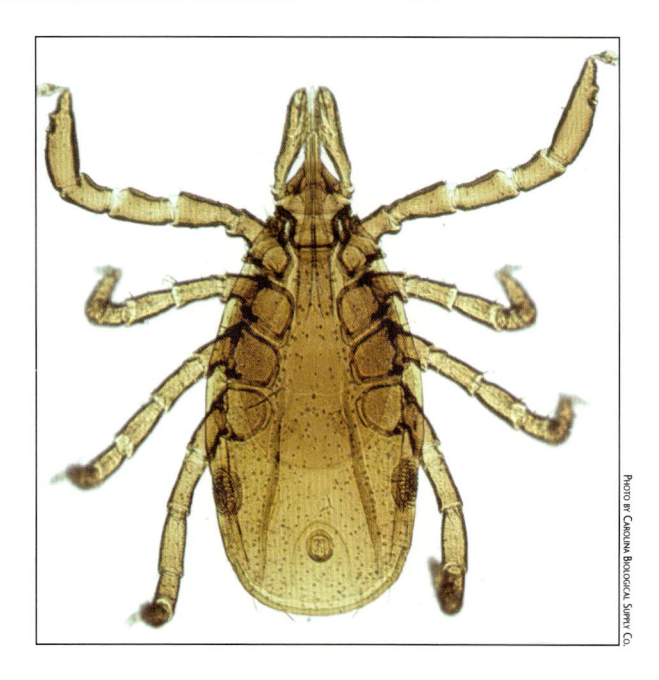

Photo by Carolina Biological Supply Co.

which may be deeply embedded in the skin. This is best accomplished with forceps designed especially for this purpose; fingers can be used but should be protected with rubber gloves, plastic wrap or at least a paper towel. The tick should be grasped as closely as possible to the animal's skin and should be pulled upward with steady, even pressure. Do not squeeze, crush or puncture the body of the tick or you risk exposure to any disease carried by that tick. Once the ticks have been removed, the sites of attachment should be disinfected. Your hands should then be washed with soap and water to further minimize risk of contagion. The tick should be disposed of in a container of alcohol or household bleach.

Some of the newer flea products, specifically those with fipronil, selamectin and permethrin, have effect against some, but not all, species of tick. Flea collars containing appropriate pesticides (e.g., propoxur, chlorfenvinphos) can aid in tick control. In most areas, such collars should be placed on animals in March, at the beginning of the tick season, and changed regularly. Leaving the collar on when the pesticide level is waning invites the development of resistance. Amitraz collars are also good for tick control, and the active ingredient does not interfere with other flea-control products. The ingredient helps prevent the attachment of ticks to the skin and will cause those ticks already on the skin to detach themselves.

TICK CONTROL
Removal of underbrush and leaf litter and the thinning of trees in areas where tick control is desired are recommended. These actions remove the cover and food sources for small animals that serve as hosts for ticks. With continued mowing of grasses in these areas, the probability of ticks' surviving is further reduced. A variety of insecticide ingredients (e.g., resmethrin, carbaryl, permethrin, chlorpyrifos, dioxathion and allethrin) are registered for tick control around the home.

MITES

Mites are tiny arachnid parasites that parasitize the skin of dogs. Skin diseases caused by mites are referred to as "mange," and there are many different forms seen in dogs. These forms are very different from one another, each one warranting an individual description.

Sarcoptic mange, or scabies, is one of the itchiest conditions that affects dogs. The microscopic *Sarcoptes* mites burrow into the superficial layers of the skin and can drive dogs crazy with itchiness. They are also communicable to people, although they can't complete their reproductive cycle on people. In addition to being tiny, the mites also are often difficult to find when trying to make a diagnosis. Skin scrapings from multiple areas are examined microscopically but, even then, sometimes the mites cannot be found.

Fortunately, scabies is relatively easy to treat, and there are a variety of products that will successfully kill the mites. Since the mites can't live in the environment for very long without feeding, a complete cure is usually possible within four to eight weeks.

Cheyletiellosis is caused by a relatively large mite, which sometimes can be seen even without a microscope. Often referred to as "walking dandruff," this also causes itching, but not usually as profound as with scabies.

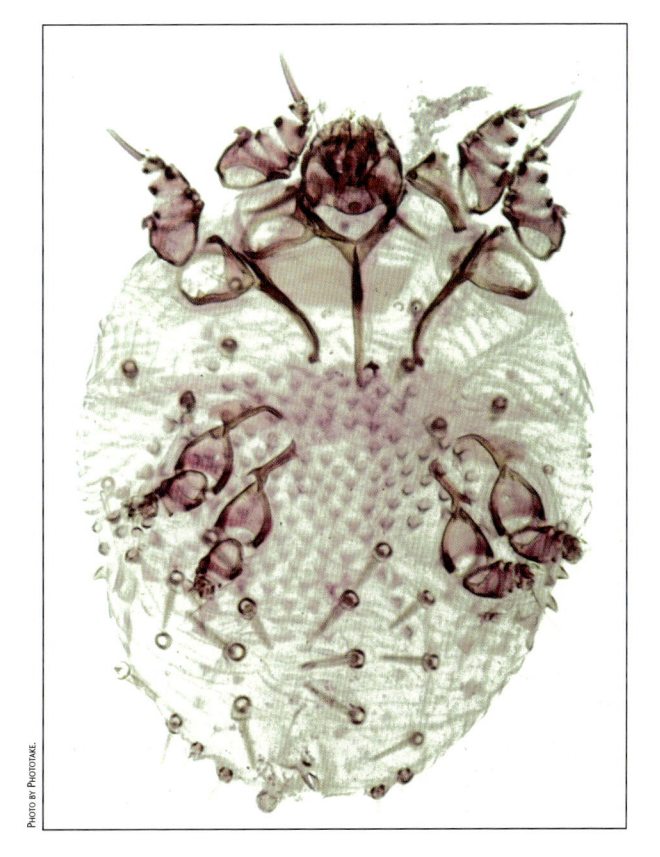

While *Cheyletiella* mites can survive somewhat longer in the environment than scabies mites, they too are relatively easy to treat, being responsive to not only the medications used to treat scabies but also often to flea-control products.

Otodectes cynotis is the canine ear mite and is one of the more common causes of mange, especially in young dogs in shelters or pet stores. That's because the mites are typically present in large numbers and are quickly spread to

Sarcoptes scabiei, commonly known as the "itch mite."

Micrograph of a dog louse, *Heterodoxus spiniger*. Female lice attach their eggs to the hairs of the dog. As the eggs hatch, the larval lice bite and feed on the blood. Lice can also feed on dead skin and hair. This feeding activity can cause hair loss and skin problems.

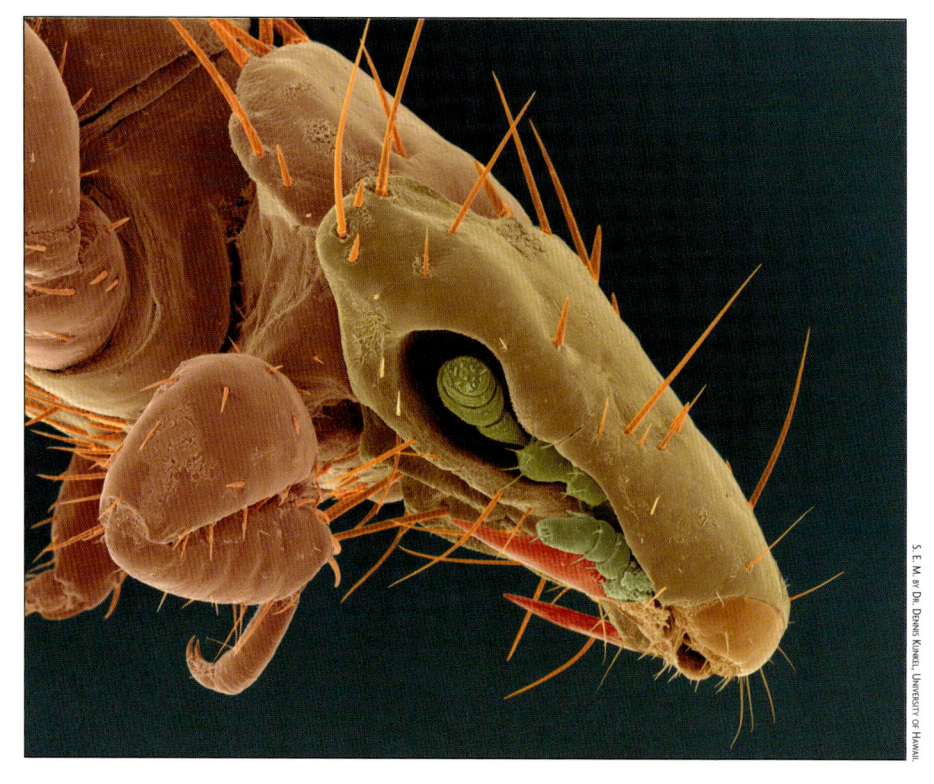

nearby animals. The mites rarely do much harm but can be difficult to eradicate if the treatment regimen is not comprehensive. While many try to treat the condition with ear drops only, this is the most common cause of treatment failure. Ear drops cause the mites to simply move out of the ears and as far away as possible (usually to the base of the tail) until the insecticide levels in the ears drop to an acceptable level—then it's back to business as usual! The successful treatment of ear mites requires treating all animals in the household with a systemic insecticide, such as selamectin, or a combination of miticidal ear drops combined with whole-body flea-control preparations.

Demodicosis, sometimes referred to as red mange, can be one of the most difficult forms of mange to treat. Part of the problem has to do with the fact that the mites live in the hair follicles and they are relatively well shielded from topical and systemic products. The main issue, however, is that demodectic mange typically results only when there is some underlying process interfering with the dog's immune system.

Since *Demodex* mites are

normal residents of the skin of mammals, including humans, there is usually a mite population explosion only when the immune system fails to keep the number of mites in check. In young animals, the immune deficit may be transient or may reflect an actual inherited immune problem. In older animals, demodicosis is usually seen only when there is another disease hampering the immune system, such as diabetes, cancer, thyroid problems or the use of immune-suppressing drugs. Accordingly, treatment involves not only trying to kill the mange mites but also discerning what is interfering with immune function and correcting it if possible.

Chiggers represent several different species of mite that don't parasitize dogs specifically, but do latch on to passersby and can cause irritation. The problem is most prevalent in wooded areas in the late summer and fall. Treatment is not difficult, as the mites do not complete their life cycle on dogs and are susceptible to a variety of miticidal products.

Mosquitoes

Mosquitoes have long been known to transmit a variety of diseases to people, as well as just being biting pests during warm weather. They also pose a real risk to pets. Not only do they carry deadly heartworms but recently there also has been much concern over their involvement with West Nile virus. While we can avoid heartworm with the use of preventive medications, there are no such preventives for West Nile virus. The only method of prevention in endemic areas is active mosquito control. Fortunately, most dogs that have been exposed to the virus only developed flu-like symptoms and, to date, there have not been the large number of reported deaths in canines as seen in some other species.

Illustration of *Demodex folliculoram*.

MOSQUITO REPELLENT

Low concentrations of DEET (less than 10%), found in many human mosquito repellents, have been safely used in dogs but, in these concentrations, probably give only about two hours of protection. DEET may be safe in these small concentrations, but since it is not licensed for use on dogs, there is no research proving its safety for dogs. Products containing permethrin give the longest-lasting protection, perhaps two to four weeks. As DEET is not licensed for use on dogs, and both DEET and permethrin can be quite toxic to cats, appropriate care should be exercised. Other products, such as those containing oil of citronella, also have some mosquito-repellent activity, but typically have a relatively short duration of action.

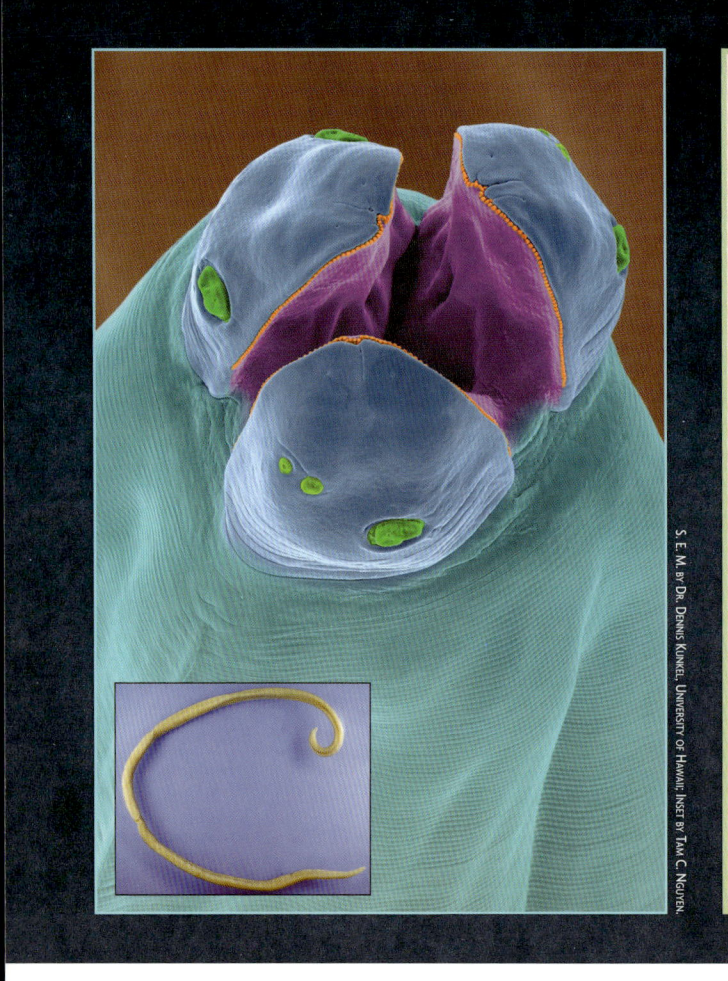

ASCARID DANGERS

The most commonly encountered worms in dogs are roundworms known as ascarids. *Toxascaris leonine* and *Toxocara canis* are the two species that infect dogs. Subsisting in the dog's stomach and intestines, adult roundworms can grow to 7 inches in length and adult females can lay in excess of 200,000 eggs in a single day.

In humans, visceral larval migrans affects people who have ingested eggs of *Toxocara canis*, which frequently contaminates children's sandboxes, beaches and park grounds. The roundworms reside in the human's stomach and intestines, as they would in a dog's, but do not mature. Instead, they find their way to the liver, lungs and skin, or even to the heart or kidneys in severe cases. Deworming puppies is critical in preventing the infection in humans, and young children should never handle nursing pups who have not been dewormed.

The ascarid roundworm *Toxocara canis*, showing the mouth with three lips. INSET: Photomicrograph of the roundworm *Ascaris lumbricoides*.

INTERNAL PARASITES: WORMS

ASCARIDS

Ascarids are intestinal roundworms that rarely cause severe disease in dogs. Nonetheless, they are of major public health significance because they can be transferred to people. Sadly, it is children who are most commonly affected by the parasite, probably from inadvertently ingesting ascarid-contaminated soil. In fact, many yards and children's sandboxes contain appreciable numbers of ascarid eggs. So, while ascarids don't bite dogs or latch onto their intestines to suck blood, they do cause some nasty medical conditions in children and are best eradicated from our furry friends. Because pups can start passing ascarid eggs by three weeks of age, most parasite-control programs begin at two weeks of age and are repeated every two weeks until pups are eight weeks old. It is important to

HOOKED ON *ANCYLOSTOMA*

Adult dogs can become infected by the bloodsucking nematodes we commonly call hookworms via ingesting larvae from the ground or via the larvae penetrating the dog's skin. It is not uncommon for infected dogs to show no symptoms of hookworm infestation. Sometimes symptoms occur within ten days of exposure. These symptoms can include bloody diarrhea, anemia, loss of weight and general weakness. Dogs pass the hookworm eggs in their stools, which serves as the vet's method of identifying the infestation. The hookworm larvae can encyst themselves in the dog's tissues and be released when the dog is experiencing stress.

Caused by an *Ancylostoma* species whose common host is the dog, cutaneous larval migrans affects humans, causing itching and lumps and streaks beneath the surface of the skin.

S.E.M. BY DR. DENNIS KUNKEL, UNIVERSITY OF HAWAII

The hookworm *Ancylostoma caninum* infests the intestines of dogs. INSET: Note the row of hooks at the posterior end, used to anchor the worm to the intestinal wall.

realize that bitches can pass ascarids to their pups even if they test negative prior to whelping. Accordingly, bitches are best treated at the same time as the pups.

HOOKWORMS

Unlike ascarids, hookworms do latch onto a dog's intestinal tract and can cause significant loss of blood and protein. Similar to ascarids, hookworms can be transmitted to humans, where they cause a condition known as cutaneous larval migrans. Dogs can become infected either by consuming the infective larvae or by the larvae's penetrating the skin directly. People most often get infected when they are lying on the ground (such as on a beach) and the larvae penetrate the skin. Yes, the larvae can penetrate through a beach blanket. Hookworms are typically susceptible to the same medications used to treat ascarids.

WHIPWORMS

Whipworms latch onto the lower aspects of the dog's colon and can cause cramping and diarrhea. Eggs do not start to appear in the dog's feces until about three months after the dog was infected. This worm has a peculiar life cycle, which makes it more difficult to control than ascarids or hookworms. The good thing is that whipworms rarely are transferred to people.

Some of the medications used to treat ascarids and hookworms are also effective against whipworms, but, in general, a separate treatment protocol is needed. Since most of the medications are effective against the adults but not the eggs or larvae, treatment is typically repeated in three weeks, and then often in three months as well. Unfortunately, since dogs don't develop resistance to whipworms, it is difficult to prevent them from getting reinfected if they visit soil contaminated with whipworm eggs.

> ### WORM-CONTROL GUIDELINES
> - Practice sanitary habits with your dog and home.
> - Clean up after your dog and don't let him sniff or eat other dogs' droppings.
> - Control insects and fleas in the dog's environment. Fleas, lice, cockroaches, beetles, mice and rats can act as hosts for various worms.
> - Prevent dogs from eating uncooked meat, raw poultry and dead animals.
> - Keep dogs and children from playing in sand and soil.
> - Kennel dogs on cement or gravel; avoid dirt runs.
> - Administer heartworm preventives regularly.
> - Have your vet examine your dog's stool at your annual visits.
> - Select a boarding kennel carefully so as to avoid contamination from other dogs or an unsanitary environment.
> - Prevent dogs from roaming. Obey local leash laws.

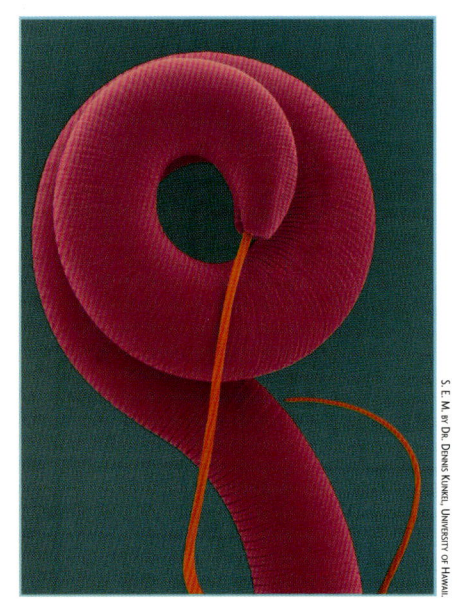

Adult whipworm, *Trichuris* sp., an intestinal parasite.

TAPEWORMS

There are many different species of tapeworm that affect dogs, but *Dipylidium caninum* is probably the most common and is spread by

Healthcare

fleas. Flea larvae feed on organic debris and tapeworm eggs in the environment and, when a dog chews at himself and manages to ingest fleas, he might get a dose of tapeworm at the same time. The tapeworm then develops further in the intestine of the dog.

The tapeworm itself, which is a parasitic flatworm that latches onto the intestinal wall, is composed of numerous segments. When the segments break off into the intestine (as proglottids), they may accumulate around the rectum, like grains of rice. While this tapeworm is disgusting in its behavior, it is not directly communicable to humans (although humans can also get infected by swallowing fleas).

A much more dangerous flatworm is *Echinococcus multilocularis*, which is typically found in foxes, coyotes and wolves. The eggs are passed in the feces and infect rodents, and, when dogs eat the rodents, the dogs can be infected by thousands of adult tapeworms. While the parasites don't cause many problems in dogs, this is considered the most lethal worm infection that people can get. Take appropriate precautions if you live in an area in which these tapeworms are found. Do not use mulch that may contain feces of dogs, cats or wildlife, and discourage your pets from hunting wildlife. Treat these tapeworm infections aggressively in pets, because if humans get infected, approximately half die.

HEARTWORMS

Heartworm disease is caused by the parasite *Dirofilaria immitis* and is seen in dogs around the world. A member of the roundworm group, it is spread between dogs by the bite of an infected mosquito. The mosquito injects infective larvae into the dog's skin with its bite, and these larvae develop under the skin for a period of time before making their way to the heart. There they develop into adults, which grow and create blockages of the heart, lungs and major blood vessels there. They also start producing offspring (microfilariae),

A dog tapeworm proglottid (body segment).

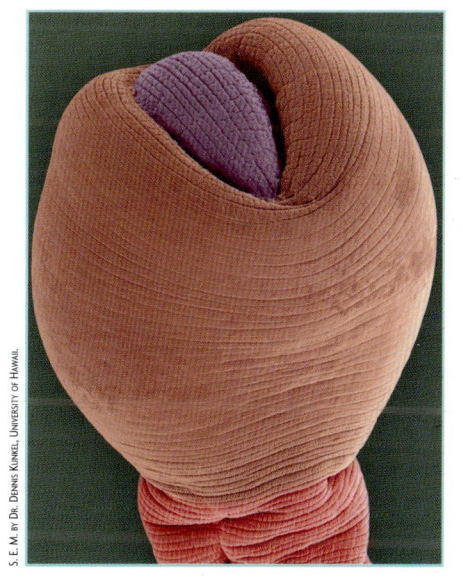

The dog tapeworm *Taenia pisiformis*.

A Look at Internal Parasites

Ascarid *Rhabditis*

Hookworm *Ancylostoma caninum*

Tapeworm *Dipylidium caninum*

Heartworm *Dirofilaria immitis*

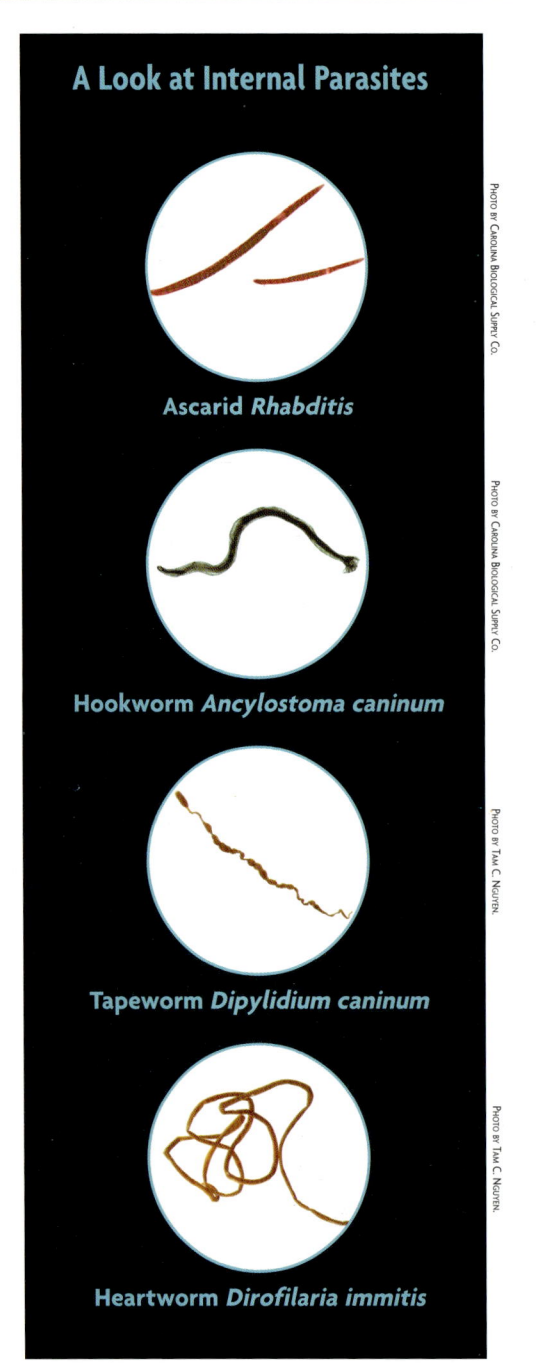

Photo by Carolina Biological Supply Co.
Photo by Carolina Biological Supply Co.
Photo by Tam C. Nguyen
Photo by Tam C. Nguyen

and these microfilariae circulate in the bloodstream, waiting to hitch a ride when the next mosquito bites. Once in the mosquito, the microfilariae develop into infective larvae and the entire process is repeated.

When dogs get infected with heartworm, over time they tend to develop symptoms associated with heart disease, such as coughing, exercise intolerance and potentially many other manifestations. Diagnosis is confirmed by either seeing the microfilariae themselves in blood samples or using immunologic tests (antigen testing) to identify the presence of adult heartworms. Since antigen tests measure the presence of adult heartworms and microfilarial tests measure offspring produced by adults, neither are positive until six to seven months after the initial infection. However, the beginning of damage can occur by fifth-stage larvae as early as three months after infection. Thus it is possible for dogs to be harboring problem-causing larvae for up to three months before either type of test would identify an infection.

The good news is that there are great protocols available for preventing heartworm in dogs. Testing is critical in the process, and it is important to understand the benefits as well as the limitations of such testing. All dogs six months of age or older that have not been on continuous heartworm-preventive medication should be

Life Cycle of the Heartworm

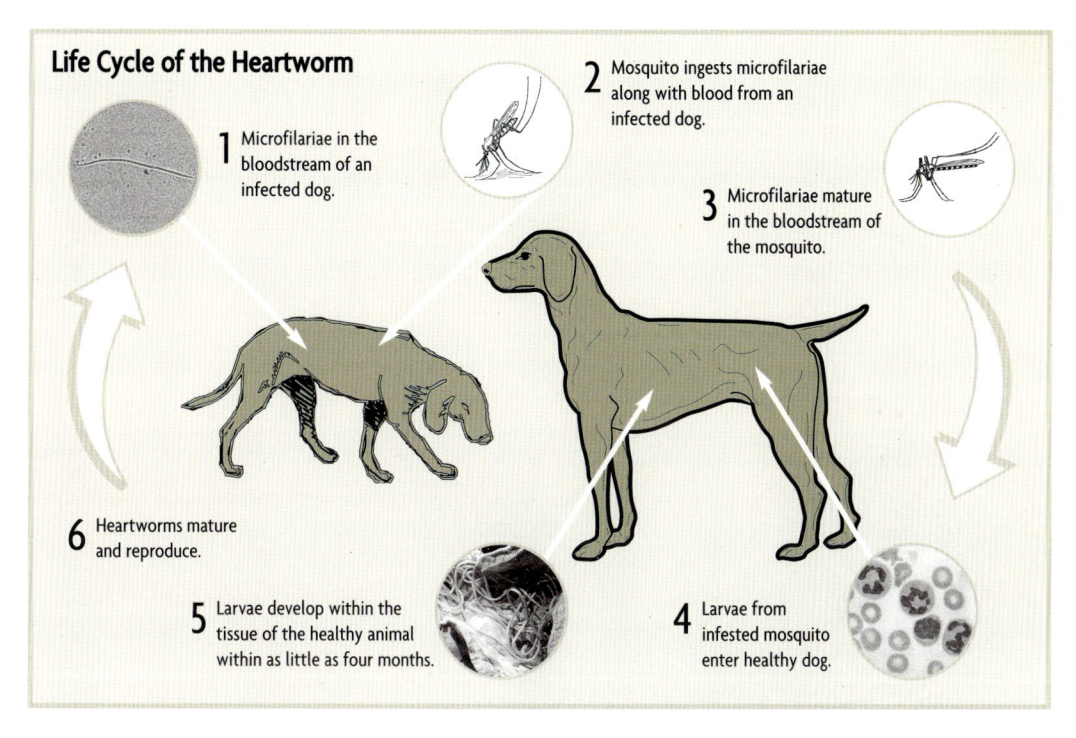

1. Microfilariae in the bloodstream of an infected dog.
2. Mosquito ingests microfilariae along with blood from an infected dog.
3. Microfilariae mature in the bloodstream of the mosquito.
4. Larvae from infested mosquito enter healthy dog.
5. Larvae develop within the tissue of the healthy animal within as little as four months.
6. Heartworms mature and reproduce.

screened with microfilarial or antigen tests. For dogs receiving preventive medication, periodic antigen testing helps assess the effectiveness of the preventives. The American Heartworm Society guidelines suggest that annual retesting may not be necessary when owners have absolutely provided continuous heartworm prevention. Retesting on a two- to three-year interval may be sufficient in these cases. However, your veterinarian will likely have specific guidelines under which heartworm preventives will be prescribed, and many prefer to err on the side of safety and retest annually.

It is indeed fortunate that heartworm is relatively easy to prevent, because treatments can be as life-threatening as the disease itself. Treatment requires a two-step process that kills the adult heartworms first and then the microfilariae. Prevention is obviously preferable; this involves a once-monthly oral or topical treatment. The most common oral preventives include ivermectin (not suitable for some breeds), moxidectin and milbemycin oxime; the once-a-month topical drug selamectin provides heartworm protection in addition to flea, some types of tick and other parasite controls.

SHOWING YOUR WIREHAIRED POINTING GRIFFON

Is dog showing in your blood? Are you excited by the idea of gaiting your handsome WPG around the ring to the thunderous applause of an enthusiastic audience? Are you certain that your beloved WPG is flawless? You are not alone! Every loving owner thinks that his dog has no faults, or too few to mention. No matter how many times an owner reads the breed standard, he cannot find any faults in his aristocratic companion dog. If this sounds like you, and if you are considering entering your WPG in a dog show, here are some basic questions to ask yourself:

- Did you purchase a "show-quality" puppy from the breeder?
- Is your puppy at least six months of age?
- Does the puppy exhibit correct show type for his breed?
- Does your puppy have any disqualifying faults?
- Is your WPG registered with the American Kennel Club?
- How much time do you have to devote to training, grooming, conditioning and exhibiting your dog?
- Do you understand the rules and regulations of a dog show?
- Do you have time to learn how to show your dog properly?
- Do you have the financial resources to invest in showing your dog?
- Will you show the dog yourself or hire a professional handler?
- Do you have a vehicle that can accommodate your weekend trips to the dog shows?

Success in the show ring requires more than a pretty face, a waggy tail and a pocketful of liver. Even though dog shows can be exciting and enjoyable, the sport of conformation makes great demands on the exhibitors and the dogs. Winning exhibitors live for their dogs, devoting time and money to

Although the dogs are lined up side-by-side, each Griff is compared to the breed standard and not the other entries. The dog that comes the closest to this ideal is selected as Best of Breed.

A successful day for Bayou Duchasseur and proud junior handler Carrie-Anne Simard.

FOR MORE INFORMATION...

For reliable up-to-date information about registration, dog shows and other canine competitions, contact one of the national registries by mail or via the Internet.

American Kennel Club
5580 Centerview Dr., Raleigh, NC 27606-3390
www.akc.org

United Kennel Club
100 E. Kilgore Road, Kalamazoo, MI 49002
www.ukcdogs.com

Canadian Kennel Club
89 Skyway Ave., Suite 100, Etobicoke, Ontario M9W 6R4 Canada
www.ckc.ca

The Kennel Club
1-5 Clarges St., Piccadilly, London
W1Y 8AB, UK
www.the-kennel-club.org.uk

their dogs' presentation, conditioning and training. Very few novices, even those with good dogs, will find themselves in the winners' circle, though it does happen. Don't be disheartened, though. Every exhibitor began as a novice and worked his way up to the Group ring. It's the "working your way up" part that you must keep in mind.

Assuming that you have purchased a puppy of the correct type and quality for showing, let's begin to examine the world of showing and what's required to get started. Although the entry fee into a dog show is nominal, there are lots of other hidden costs involved with "finishing" your WPG, that is, making him a champion. Things like equipment, travel, training and conditioning all cost money. A more serious campaign will include fees for a professional handler, boarding, cross-country travel and advertising. Top-winning show dogs can represent a very considerable investment—over $100,000 has been spent in campaigning some dogs. (The investment can be less, of course, for owners who don't use professional handlers.)

Many owners, on the other hand, enter their "average" WPGs in dog shows for the fun and enjoyment of it. Dog showing makes an absorbing hobby, with many rewards for dogs and owners alike. If you're having fun, meeting other people who share your interests and enjoying the overall experience, you likely will catch the "bug." Once the dog-show bug bites, its effects can last a lifetime; it's certainly much better than a deer tick! Soon you will be envisioning yourself in the center ring at the Westminster Kennel Club Dog Show in New York City, competing for the prestigious Best in Show cup. This magical dog show is televised annually from Madison Square Garden, and the victorious dog becomes a celebrity overnight.

AKC CONFORMATION SHOWING

GETTING STARTED

Visiting a dog show as a spectator is a great place to start. Pick up the show catalog to find out what time your breed is being shown, who is judging the breed and in which ring the classes will be held. To start, WPGs compete against other WPGs, and the winner is selected as Best of Breed by the judge. This is the procedure for each breed. At a group show, all of the Best of Breed winners go on to compete for Group One (first place) in their respective groups. For example, all Best of Breed winners in a given group compete against each other; this is done for all seven groups. Finally, all seven group winners go head to head in the ring for the Best in Show award.

What most spectators don't understand is the basic idea of conformation. A dog show is often referred as a "conformation" show. This means that the judge should decide how each dog stacks up

Practice makes perfect. This proud owner helps his Griff demonstrate how he "stacks" up against the competition.

Showing

(conforms) to the breed standard for his given breed: how well does this WPG conform to the ideal representative detailed in the standard? Ideally, this is what happens. In reality, however, this ideal often gets slighted as the judge compares WPG #1 to WPG #2. Again, the ideal is that each dog is judged based on his merits in comparison to his breed standard, not in comparison to the other dogs in the ring. It is easier for judges to compare dogs of the same breed to decide which they think is the better specimen; in the Group and Best in Show ring, however, it is very difficult to compare one breed to another, like apples to oranges. Thus the dog's conformation to the breed standard—not to mention advertising dollars and good handling—is essential to success in conformation shows. The dog described in the standard (the standard for each AKC breed is written and approved by the breed's national parent club and then submitted to the AKC for approval) is the perfect dog of that breed, and breeders keep their eye on the standard when they choose which dogs to breed, hoping to get closer and closer to the ideal with each litter.

Another good first step for the novice is to join a dog club. You

> **MEET THE AKC**
> The American Kennel Club is the main governing body of the dog sport in the United States. Founded in 1884, the AKC consists of 500 or more independent dog clubs plus 4,500 affiliated clubs, all of which follow the AKC rules and regulations. Additionally, the AKC maintains a registry for pure-bred dogs in the US and works to preserve the integrity of the sport and its continuation in the country. Over 1,000,000 dogs are registered each year, representing about 150 recognized breeds. There are over 15,000 competitive events held annually for which over 2,000,000 dogs enter to participate. Dogs compete to earn over 40 different titles, from Champion to Companion Dog to Master Agility Champion.

Each Griff is gaited so that the judge can evaluate movement. Ideally the breed should have a smooth, powerful and ground-covering gait.

WIREHAIRED POINTING GRIFFON

> **BECOMING A CHAMPION**
> An official AKC championship of record requires that a dog accumulate 15 points under 3 different judges, including 2 "majors" under different judges. Points are awarded based on the number of dogs entered into competition, varying from breed to breed and place to place. A win of three, four or five points is considered a "major." The AKC annually assigns a schedule of points to adjust for variations that accompany a breed's popularity and the population of a given area.

will be astonished by the many and different kinds of dog clubs in the country, with about 5,000 clubs holding events every year. Most clubs require that prospective new members present two letters of recommendation from existing members. Perhaps you've made some friends visiting a show held by a particular club and you would like to join that club. Dog clubs may specialize in a single breed, like a local or regional WPG club, or in a specific pursuit, such as obedience, tracking or hunting tests. There are all-breed clubs for all dog enthusiasts; they sponsor special training days, seminars on topics like grooming or handling or lectures on breeding or canine genetics. There are also clubs that specialize in certain types of dogs, like herding dogs, hunting dogs, companion dogs, etc.

A parent club is the national organization, sanctioned by the AKC, which promotes and safeguards its breed in the country. The American Wirehaired Pointing Griffon Association was formed in 1991 and can be contacted on the Internet at www.awpga.com. The parent club holds an annual national specialty show, usually in a different city each year, in which many of the country's top dogs, handlers and breeders gather to compete. At a specialty show, only members of a single breed are invited to participate. There are also group specialties, in which all members of a group are invited. For more information about dog clubs in your area, contact the AKC at www.akc.org on the Internet or write them at their Raleigh, NC address.

How Shows Are Organized

Three kinds of conformation shows are offered by the AKC. There is the all-breed show, in which all AKC-recognized breeds can compete; the specialty show, which is for one breed only and usually sponsored by the breed's parent club; and the group show, for all breeds in one of the AKC's seven groups. The WPG competes in the Sporting Group.

For a dog to become an AKC champion of record, the dog must earn 15 points at shows. The points must be awarded by at least three different judges and must include two "majors" under different judges. A "major" is a three-, four- or five-point win, and the number of points per win is determined by the number of dogs competing in the show on that day. (Dogs that are absent or are excused are not counted.) The number of points that are awarded varies from breed to breed. More dogs are needed to attain a major in more popular breeds, and fewer dogs are needed in less popular breeds. Yearly, the AKC evaluates the number of dogs in competition in each division (there are 14 divisions in all, based on geography) and may or may not change the numbers of dogs required for each number of points. For example, a major in Division 2 (Delaware, New Jersey and Pennsylvania) recently required 17 dogs or 16 bitches for a 3-point major, 29 dogs or 27 bitches for a 4-point major and 51 dogs or 46 bitches for a 5-point major. The WPG attracts numerically proportionate representation at all-breed shows.

Only one dog and one bitch of each breed can win points at a given show. There are no "co-ed" classes except for champions of record. Dogs and bitches do not compete against each other until they are champions. Dogs that are not champions (referred to as "class dogs") compete in one of five classes. The class in which a dog is entered depends on age and previous show wins. First there is the Puppy Class (sometimes divided further into classes for 6- to 9-month-olds and 9- to 12-month-olds); next is the Novice Class (for dogs that have no points toward their championships and whose only first-place wins have come in the Puppy Class or the Novice

SHOW POTENTIAL
How possible is it to predict how your ten-week-old puppy will eventually do in the show ring? Most show dogs reach their prime at around three years of age, when their bodies are physically mature and their coats are in "full bloom." Experienced breeders, having watched countless pups grow into Best of Breed winners, recognize the glowing attributes that spell "show potential." When selecting a puppy for show, it's best to trust the breeder to recommend which puppy will best suit your aspirations. Some breeders recommend starting with a male puppy, which likely will be more "typey" than his female counterpart.

WIREHAIRED POINTING GRIFFON

Class, the latter class limited to three first places); then there is the American-bred Class (for dogs bred in the US); the Bred-by-Exhibitor Class (for dogs handled by their breeders or by immediate family members of their breeders); and the Open Class (for any non-champions). Any dog may enter the Open Class, regardless of age or win history, but to be competitive the dog should be older and have ring experience.

The judge at the show begins judging the male dogs in the Puppy Class(es) and proceeds through the other classes. The judge awards first through fourth place in each class. The first-place winners of each class then compete with one another in the Winners Class to determine Winners Dog. The judge then starts over with the bitches, beginning with the Puppy Class(es) and proceeding up to the Winners Class to award Winners Bitch, just as he did with the dogs. A Reserve Winners Dog and Reserve Winners Bitch are also selected; they could be awarded the points in the case of a disqualification.

The Winners Dog and Winners Bitch are the two that are awarded the points for their breed. They

A wonderful representation of the breed, this Griff receives his ribbon with pride as Best of Breed at a dog show.

then go on to compete with any champions of record (often called "specials") of their breed that are entered in the show. The champions may be dogs or bitches; in this class, all are shown together. The judge reviews the Winners Dog and Winners Bitch along with all of the champions to select the Best of Breed winner. The Best of Winners is selected between the Winners Dog and Winners Bitch; if one of these two is selected Best of Breed as well, he or she is automatically determined Best of Winners. Lastly, the judge selects Best of Opposite Sex to the Best of Breed winner. The Best of Breed winner then goes on to the Group competition.

At a group or all-breed show, the Best of Breed winners from each breed are divided into their respective groups to compete against one another for Group One through Group Four. Group One (first place) is awarded to the dog that best lives up to the ideal for his breed as described in the standard. A group judge, therefore, must have a thorough working knowledge of many breed standards. After placements have been made in each group, the seven Group One winners (from the Sporting Group, Toy Group, Hound Group, etc.) compete against each other for the top honor, Best in Show.

There are different ways to find out about dog shows in your area. The American Kennel Club's monthly magazine, the *American*

> **FIVE CLASSES AT SHOWS**
> At most AKC all-breed shows, there are five regular classes offered: Puppy, Novice, Bred-by-Exhibitor, American-bred and Open. The Puppy Class is usually divided as 6 to 9 months of age and 9 to 12 months of age. When deciding in which class to enter your dog, whether male or female, you must carefully check the show schedule to make sure that you have selected the right class. Depending on the age of the dog, its previous first-place wins and the sex of the dog, you must make the best choice. It is possible to enter a one-year-old dog who has not won sufficient first places in any of the non-Puppy Classes, though the competition is more intense the further you progress from the Puppy Class.

Kennel Gazette, is accompanied by the *Events Calendar;* this magazine is available through subscription. You can also look on the AKC's and your parent club's websites for information and check the event listings in your local newspaper.

Your WPG must be six months of age or older and registered with the AKC in order to be entered in AKC-sanctioned shows in which there are classes for the WPG. Your WPG also must not possess any disqualifying faults and must be sexually intact. The reason for the latter is simple: dog shows are the proving grounds to determine

Flying high. The Griff's natural athleticism and trainability give him the potential for success in many areas of the dog sport.

which dogs and bitches are worthy of being bred. If they cannot be bred, that defeats the purpose! On that note, only dogs that have achieved championships, thus proving their excellent quality, should be bred. If you have spayed or neutered your dog, however, there are many AKC events other than conformation, such as obedience trials, agility trials and the Canine Good Citizen® Program, in which you and your WPG can participate.

OTHER TYPES OF COMPETITION

In addition to conformation shows, the AKC holds a variety of other competitive events. Obedience trials, agility trials and tracking trials are open to all breeds, while hunting tests, field trials, lure coursing, herding tests and trials, earthdog tests and coonhound events are limited to specific breeds or groups of breeds. The Junior Showmanship program is offered to aspiring young handlers and their dogs, and the Canine Good Citizen® Program is an all-around good-behavior test open to all dogs, purebred and mixed.

OBEDIENCE TRIALS

Mrs. Helen Whitehouse Walker, a Standard Poodle fancier, can be credited with introducing obedience trials to the United States. In the 1930s she designed a series of exercises based on those of the Associated Sheep, Police, Army Dog Society of Great Britain. These exercises were intended to evaluate the working relationship between dog and owner. Since those early days of the sport in the US, obedience trials have grown more and more popular, and now more than 2,000 trials each year attract over 100,000 dogs and their owners. Any dog registered with the AKC, regardless of neutering or other disqualifications that would preclude entry in conformation competition, can participate in obedience trials.

There are three levels of difficulty in obedience competition. The first (and easiest) level is the Novice, in which dogs can earn the Companion Dog (CD) title. The

Showing

intermediate level is the Open level, in which the Companion Dog Excellent (CDX) title is awarded. The advanced level is the Utility level, in which dogs compete for the Utility Dog (UD) title. Classes at each level are further divided into "A" and "B," with "A" for beginners and "B" for those with more experience. In order to win a title at a given level, a dog must earn three "legs." A "leg" is accomplished when a dog scores 170 or higher (200 is a perfect score). The scoring system gets a little trickier when you understand that a dog must score more than 50% of the points available for each exercise in order to actually earn the points. Available points for each exercise range between 20 and 40.

A dog must complete different exercises at each level of obedience. The Novice exercises are the easiest, with the Open and finally the Utility levels progressing in difficulty. Examples of Novice exercises are on- and off-lead heeling, a figure-8 pattern, performing a recall (or come), long sit, long down and standing for examination. In the Open level, the Novice-level exercises are required again, but this time without a leash and for longer durations. In addition, the dog must clear a broad jump, retrieve over a jump and drop on recall. In the Utility level, the exercises are quite difficult, including executing basic commands based on hand signals, following a complex heeling

Agility competition is fast-paced and fun, with plenty of running, jumping and other tests of the dog's coordination. This Griff is obviously enjoying himself while following his handler's directions.

WIREHAIRED POINTING GRIFFON

A WPG sails through a jump during an agility trial. There isn't much that this versatile gundog can't do.

pattern, locating articles based on scent discrimination and completing jumps at the handler's direction.

Once he's earned the UD title, a dog can go on to win the prestigious title of Utility Dog Excellent (UDX) by winning "legs" in ten shows. Additionally, Utility Dogs who win "legs" in Open B and Utility B earn points toward the lofty title of Obedience Trial Champion (OTCh.). Established in 1977 by the AKC, this title requires a dog to earn 100 points as well as three first places in a combination of Open B and Utility B classes under three different judges. The "brass ring" of obedience competition is the AKC's National Obedience Invitational. This is an exclusive competition for only the cream of the obedience crop. In order to qualify for the invitational, a dog must be ranked in either the top 25 all-breeds in obedience or in the top three for his breed in obedience. The title at stake here is that of National Obedience Champion (NOC).

AGILITY TRIALS

Agility trials became sanctioned by the AKC in August 1994, when the first licensed agility trials were held. Since that time, agility certainly has grown in popularity by leaps and bounds, literally! The AKC allows all registered breeds (including Miscellaneous Class breeds) to participate, providing the dog is 12 months of age or older. Agility is designed so that the handler demonstrates how well the dog can work at his side. The handler directs his dog through, over, under and around an obstacle course that includes jumps, tires, the dog walk, weave poles, pipe tunnels, collapsed tunnels and more. While working his way through the course, the dog must keep one eye and ear on the handler and the rest of his body on the course. The handler runs along with the dog, giving verbal and hand signals to guide the dog through the course.

The first organization to promote agility trials in the US was the United States Dog Agility

Showing

Despite his impressive ability in many kinds of competitive events, the Griff is happiest spending the day hunting in the field with his owner.

WIREHAIRED POINTING GRIFFON

Association, Inc. (USDAA). Established in 1986, the USDAA sparked the formation of many member clubs around the country. To participate in USDAA trials, dogs must be at least 18 months of age.

The USDAA and AKC both offer titles to winning dogs, although the exercises and requirements of the two organizations differ. Agility Dog (AD), Advanced Agility Dog (AAD) and Master Agility Dog (MAD) are the titles offered by the USDAA, while the AKC offers Novice Agility (NA), Open Agility (OA), Agility Excellent (AX) and Master Agility Excellent (MX). Beyond these four AKC titles, dogs can win additional titles in "jumper" classes: Jumper with Weave Novice (NAJ), Open (OAJ) and Excellent (MXJ). The ultimate title in AKC agility is MACH, Master Agility Champion. Dogs can continue to add number designations to the MACH title,

A little bit tousled, a little bit tired—but still plenty game for the game.

UKC POINTING DOG PROGRAM

The United Kennel Club (UKC) offers a Pointing Dog Program that is based on European-style hunting events, combining elements of field trials and hunt tests. These walking trials are aimed at companion bird dogs and are essentially non-competitive, nurturing an atmosphere of good sportsmanship and learning. Hunters and their dogs are encouraged to participate in these rewarding events.

All pointing breeds are evaluated according to breed type. There are two divisions: Novice and Open, and professional handlers are only permitted if they are handling their own dogs. Novice dogs run in solo heats and are not required to be steady to wing and shot. Dogs in the Open division may be run in braces (pairs). Dogs up to three years of age are rewarded for natural ability and receive certificates.

indicating how many times the dog has met the title's requirements (MACH1, MACH2 and so on).

Agility trials are a great way to keep your dog active, and they will keep you running, too! You should join a local agility club to learn more about the sport. These clubs offer sessions in which you can introduce your dog to the various obstacles as well as training classes to prepare him for competition. In no time, your dog will be climbing A-frames, crossing the dog walk and flying over hurdles, all with you right beside him. Your heart will leap every time your dog jumps through the hoop—and you'll be having just as much (if not more) fun!

TRACKING

Tracking tests are exciting ways to test your WPG's instinctive scenting ability on a competitive level. All dogs have a nose, and all breeds are welcome in tracking tests. The first AKC-licensed tracking test took place in 1937 as part of the Utility level at an obedience trial, and thus competitive tracking was officially begun. The first title, Tracking Dog (TD), was offered in 1947, ten years after the first official tracking test. It was not until 1980 that the AKC added the title Tracking Dog Excellent (TDX), which was followed by the title Variable Surface Tracking (VST) in 1995. Champion Tracker (CT) is awarded to a dog who has earned all three of those titles.

The TD level is the first and most basic level in tracking, progressing in difficulty to the TDX and then the VST. A dog must follow a track laid by a human 30 to 120 minutes prior in order to earn the TD title. The track is about 500 yards long and contains up to 5 directional changes. At the next level, the TDX, the dog must follow a 3- to 5-hour-old track over a course that is up to 1,000 yards long and has up to 7 directional changes. In the most difficult level, the VST, the track is up to 5 hours old and located in an urban setting.

"What's next?" This athletic breed is always up for an exciting activity.

FIELD TRIALS

Field trials are offered to the retrievers, pointers and spaniel breeds of the Sporting Group as well as to the Beagles, Dachshunds and Bassets of the Hound Group. The purpose of field trials is to demonstrate a dog's ability to perform his breed's original purpose in the field. The events vary depending on the type of dog, but in all trials dogs compete against one another for placement and for points toward their Field Champion (FC) titles. Dogs that earn their FC titles plus their championship in the conformation ring are known as Dual Champions; this is extremely prestigious, as it shows that the dog is the ideal blend of form and function, excelling in both areas.

Retriever field trials, designed to simulate "an ordinary day's shoot," are popular and likely the most demanding of these trials. Dogs must "mark" the location of downed feathered game and then

PARTICIPATING IN NAVHDA HUNTING TESTS

The North American Versatile Hunting Dog Association (NAVHDA) assists hunters in training their dogs to be "useful, productive hunting companions" and to provide sportsmen with standard methods of evaluating versatile hunting dogs. According to the purpose as stated by NAVHDA, "The organization is dedicated to fostering, improving, promoting, and protecting the versatile hunting dog in North America. Underlying these aims is the desire to serve the interests of game conservation, prevention of cruelty to animals, and the gun dog hunter by helping the hunter to train his dog to work before and after the shot, on land and in water."

In order to participate in a NAVHDA test, the dog must be registered with NAVHDA and you must be a member as well. Since 1969 NAVHDA has offered comprehensive tests for versatile hunting dogs. Today NAVHDA offers four types of hunting tests: natural ability test, aimed at evaluating inherited abilities of young dogs (up to 16 months of age); utility preparatory test, geared toward gauging a dog's development on his way to the utility test; utility test, aimed at evaluating the excellence of field- and water-trained dogs; and the invitational test, intended only for the most highly trained and skilled versatile hunters to test their ability in advanced gundog work. The tests are conducted in environments that simulate actual hunting conditions. Each dog entered is evaluated by three judges, scoring the dogs against a standard not against each other (excepting the invitational level where dogs are trialed in hunting pairs).

A monthly magazine published by NAVHDA for all its members, *Versatile Hunting Dog* includes informative articles about hunting, training, trialing and much more. The organization is based in Arlington Heights, Idaho and can be contacted online at www.navhda.org.

return the birds to the shooter. Successful dogs are able to "mark" the downed game by remembering where the bird fell as well as correct use of the wind and terrain. Dogs are tested both on land and in water.

Difficulty levels are based on the number of birds downed as well as the number of "blind retrieves" (where a bird is placed away from the view of the dog and the handler directs the dog by the use of hand signals and verbal commands). The term "Non-Slip" retriever, often applied to these trials, refers to a dog that is steady at the handler's side until commanded to go. Every field trial includes four stakes of increasing levels of difficulty. Each stake is judged by a team of two judges who look for many natural abilities, including steadiness, courage, style, control and training.

HUNTING TESTS

Hunting tests are not competitive like field trials, and participating dogs are judged against a standard, as in a conformation show. The first hunting tests were devised by the North American Hunting Retriever Association (NAHRA) as an alternative to field trials for retriever owners to appreciate their dogs' natural innate ability in the field without the expense and pressure of a formal field trial. The intent of hunting tests is the same as that of field trials: to test the dog's ability in a simulated hunting scenario.

The AKC instituted its hunting tests in June 1985; since then, their popularity has grown tremendously. The AKC offers three titles at hunting tests, Junior Hunter (JH), Senior Hunter (SH) and Master Hunter (MH). Each title requires that the dog earn qualifying "legs" at the tests: the JH requiring four; the SH, five; and the MH, six. In addition to the AKC, the United Kennel Club (UKC) also offers hunting tests through its affiliate club, the Hunting Retriever Club, Inc. (HRC), which began the tests in 1984.

In the field, the Griff is the paragon of hunting prowess with skills much appreciated by hunters; they don't call this breed the "supreme gundog" for nothing.

BEHAVIOR OF YOUR WIREHAIRED POINTING GRIFFON

You chose your dog because something clicked the minute you set eyes on him. Or perhaps it seemed that the dog selected you and that's what clinched the deal. Either way, you are now investing time and money in this dog, a true pal and an outstanding member of the family. Everything about him is perfect…well, almost perfect. Remember, he is a dog! For that matter, how does he think *you're* doing?

UNDERSTANDING THE CANINE MINDSET

For starters, you and your dog are on different wavelengths. Your dog is similar to a toddler in that both live in the present tense only. A dog's view of life is based primarily on cause and effect, which is similar to the old saying, "Nothing teaches a youngster to hang on like falling off the swing." If your dog stumbles down a flight of three steps, the next time he will try the Superman approach and fling himself off the top one!

Your dog makes connections based on the fact that he lives in the present, so when he is doing something and you interrupt to dispense praise or a correction, a connection, positive or negative, is made. To the dog, that's like one plus one equals two! In the same sense, it's also easy to see that when your timing is off, you will cause an incorrect connection. The

SPLASH!

Not every dog knows how to swim. If your dog is afraid of water, you can help him get over his fear and learn to swim. Start by holding him securely around his ribs in calm water. Let him "dog paddle," but don't let go. Keep practicing. Whether he learns to like water or continues to hate it, you will need to watch him near water as you would a toddler. Your Griff will not likely need much encouragement, as the breed is a natural and skilled water retriever.

one-plus-one way of thinking is why you must never scold a dog for behavior that took place an hour, 15 minutes or even 5 seconds ago. But it is also why, when your timing is perfect, you can teach him to do all kinds of wonderful things—as soon as he has made that essential connection. What helps the process is his desire to please you and to have your approval.

There are behaviors we admire in dogs, such as friendliness and obedience, as well as those behaviors that cause problems to a varying degree. The dog owner who encounters minor behavioral problems is wise to solve them promptly or get professional help. Bad behaviors are not corrected by repeatedly shouting "No" or getting angry with the dog. Only the giving of praise and approval for good behavior lets your dog understand right from wrong. The longer a bad behavior is allowed to continue, the harder it is to overcome. A responsible breeder is often able to help. Each dog is unique, so try not to compare your dog's behavior with your neighbor's dog or the one you had as a child.

Have your veterinarian check the dog to see whether a behavior problem could have a physical cause. An earache or toothache, for example, could be the reason for a dog to snap at you if you were to touch his head when putting on his leash. A sharp correction from you would only increase the behavior. When a physical basis is eliminated, and if the problem is not something you understand or can cope with, ask for the name of a behavioral specialist, preferably one who is familiar with the WPG. Be sure to keep the breeder informed of your progress.

Many things, such as environment and inherited traits, form the basic behavior of a dog, just as in humans. You also must factor into his temperament the purpose for which your dog was originally bred. The major obstacle lies in the dog's inability to explain his behavior to us in a way that we understand. The one thing you should not do is to give up and abandon your dog. Somewhere a misunderstanding has occurred, but with help and patient understanding on your part, you

Dogs can develop unforeseen habits. Some like to be where the action is and are always snooping around.

When still with the breeder, littermates do everything together, and they will miss that companionship initially when they go to their new homes.

should be able to work out the majority of bothersome behaviors.

AGGRESSION

"Aggression" is a word that is often misunderstood and is sometimes even used to describe what is actually normal canine behavior. For example, it's normal for puppies to growl when playing tug-of-war. It's puppy talk. There are different forms of dog aggression, but all are degrees of dominance, indicating that the dog, not his master, is (or thinks he is) in control. When the dog feels that he (or his control of the situation) is threatened, he will respond. The extent of aggressive behavior, if it occurs at all, varies with individual dogs within any breed. It is not at all pleasant to see bared teeth or to hear your dog growl or snarl, but these are signs of behavior that, if left uncorrected, can become extremely dangerous. A word of warning here: never challenge an aggressive dog. He is unpredictable and therefore unreliable to approach.

Nothing gets a "hello" from strangers on the street quicker than walking a puppy, but people should ask permission before petting your dog so you can tell him to sit in order to receive the admiring pats. If a hand comes down over the dog's head and he shrinks back, ask the person to bring his hand up, underneath the pup's chin. Now you're correcting strangers, too! But if you don't, it could make your dog afraid of strangers, which in turn can lead to fear-biting. Socialization prevents much aggression before it rears its ugly head.

The body language of an aggressive dog about to attack is clear. The dog will have a hard,

DOMINANCE

Dogs are born with dominance skills, meaning that they can be quite clever in trying to get their way. The "follow-me" trot to the cookie jar is an example. The toy dropped in your lap says "Play with me." The leash delivered to you along with an excited look means "Take me for a walk." These are all good-natured dominant behaviors. Ask your dog to sit before agreeing to his request and you'll remain "top dog."

steady stare. He will try to look as big as possible by standing stiff-legged, pushing out his chest, keeping his ears up and holding his tail up and steady. The hackles on his back will rise so that a ridge of hairs stands up. This posture may include the curled lip, snarl and/or growl, or he may be silent. He looks, and definitely is, very dangerous.

This dominant posture is seen in dogs that are territorially aggressive. Deliverymen are constant victims of serious bites from such dogs. Territorial aggression is the reason you should never, ever try to train a puppy to be a watchdog. It can escalate into this type of behavior over which you will have no control. All forms of aggression must be taken seriously and dealt with immediately. If signs of aggressive behavior continue, or grow worse, or if you are at all unsure about how to deal with your dog's behavior, get the help of a professional.

Uncontrolled aggression, sometimes called "irritable aggression," is not something for the pet owner to try to solve. If you cannot solve your dog's dangerous behavior with professional help, and you (quite rightly) do not wish to keep a canine time-bomb in your home, you will have some important decisions to make. Aggressive dogs often cannot be rehomed successfully, as they are dangerous and unreliable in their

Dog-aggression should not be an issue in the WPG if introductions are done with care and the dogs are supervised as the friendship develops.

behavior. An aggressive dog should be dealt with only by someone who knows exactly the situation that he is getting into and has the experience, dedication and ideal living environment to attempt rehabilitating the dog, which often is not possible. In these cases, the dog ends up having to be humanely put down. Making a decision about euthanasia is not an easy undertaking for anyone, for any reason, but you cannot pass on to another home a dog that you know could cause harm.

A milder form of aggression is the dog's guarding anything that he perceives to be his—his food dish, his toys, his bed and/or his crate. This can be prevented if you take firm control from the start. The young puppy can and should be taught that his leader will share, but that certain rules apply. Guarding is mild aggression only in the beginning stages, and it will worsen and become dangerous if you let it.

Don't try to snatch anything away from your puppy. Bargain for the item in question so that you can positively reinforce him when he gives it up. Punishment only results in worsening any aggressive behavior.

SEPARATION ANXIETY
Any behaviorist will tell you that separation anxiety is the most common problem about which pet owners complain. It is also one of the easiest to prevent. Unfortunately, a behaviorist usually is not consulted until the dog is a stressed-out, neurotic mess. At that stage, it is indeed a problem that requires the help of a professional.

Training the puppy to the fact that people in the house come and go is essential in order to avoid this anxiety. Leaving the puppy in his crate or a confined area while family members go in and out, and stay out for longer and longer periods of time, is the basic way to desensitize the pup to the family's frequent departures. If you are at home most of every day, make it a point to go out for at least an hour or two whenever possible.

Alone in the fenced yard is not the answer to your WPG's exercise needs; he thrives on varied activities and plenty of interaction with his owners.

Behavior

I CAN'T SMILE WITHOUT YOU

How can you tell whether your dog is suffering from separation anxiety? Not every dog who enjoys a close bond with his owner will suffer from separation anxiety. In actuality, only a small percentage of dogs are affected. Separation anxiety manifests itself in dogs older than one year of age and may not occur until the dog is a senior. A number of destructive behaviors are associated with the problem, including scratch marks in front of doorways, bite marks on furniture, drool stains on furniture and flooring and tattered draperies, carpets or cushions. The most reliable sign of separation anxiety is howling and crying when the owner leaves and then barking like mad for extended periods. Affected dogs may also defecate or urinate throughout the home, attempt to escape when the door opens, vocalize excessively and show signs of depression (including loss of appetite, listlessness and lack of activity).

in the morning that they're off to school until afternoon. Lipstick? Aftershave lotion? Lunch boxes? Every move you make registers in his sensory perception and memory. Your puppy knows more about your departures than you do. You can't get away with a thing!

Before you got dressed, you checked the dog's water bowl and his supply of long-lasting chew toys and turned the radio on low. You will leave him in what he considers his "safe" area, not with total freedom of the house. If

How you leave is vital to the dog's reaction. Your dog is no fool. He knows the difference between sweats and business suits, jeans and dresses. He sees you pat your pocket to check for your wallet, open your briefcase, check that you have your cell phone or pick up the car keys. He knows from the hurry of the kids

Praise and petting are a big part of forming a bond with your dog and rewarding him for appropriate behavior.

Every WPG's personality is different. Generalizations can be made about the breed's overall temperament, but each dog is an individual with his own likes and dislikes.

you've invested in child safety gates, you can be reasonably sure that he'll remain in the designated area. Don't give him access to a window where he can watch you leave the house. If you're leaving for an hour or two, just put him into his crate with a safe toy.

Now comes the test. You are ready to walk out the door. Do not give your WPG a big hug and a fond farewell. Do not drag out a long goodbye. Those are the very things that jump-start separation anxiety. Toss a biscuit into the dog's area, call out "So long, pooch" and close the door. You're gone. The chances are that the dog may bark a couple of times, or maybe whine once or twice, and then settle down to enjoy his biscuit and take a lovely nap, especially if you took him for a nice long walk after breakfast. As he grows up, the barks and whines will stop because it's an old routine, so why should he make the effort?

When you first brought home the puppy, the come-and-go routine was intermittent and constant. He was put into his crate with a tiny treat. You left (silently) and returned in 3 minutes, then 5, then 10, then 15, then half an hour, until finally you could leave without a problem and be gone for 2 or 3 hours. If, at any time in the future, there's a "separation" problem, refresh his memory by going back to that basic training.

Now comes the next most important part—your return. Do not make a big production of coming home. "Hi, poochie" is as grand a greeting as he needs. When you've taken off your hat and coat, tossed your briefcase on the hall table and glanced at the mail, and the dog has settled down from the excitement of seeing you "in person" from his confined area, then go and give him a warm, friendly greeting. A potty trip is needed and a walk would be appreciated, since he's been such a good dog.

CHEWING

All puppies chew. All dogs chew. This is a fact of life for canines, and sometimes you may think it's what your dog does best! A pup starts chewing when his first set of teeth erupts and continues throughout the teething period. Chewing gives the pup relief from itchy gums and incoming teeth and, from that time on, he gets great satisfaction out of this normal, somewhat idle, canine activity. Providing safe chew toys is the best way to direct this behavior in an appropriate manner. Chew toys are available in all sizes, textures and flavors, but you must monitor the wear-and-tear inflicted on your pup's toys to be sure that the ones you've chosen are safe and remain in good condition.

Puppies cannot distinguish between a rawhide toy and a nice leather shoe or wallet. It's up to you to keep your possessions away from the dog and to keep your eye on the dog. There's a form of destruction caused by chewing that is not the dog's fault. Let's say you allow him on the sofa. One day he takes a rawhide bone up on the sofa and, in the course of chewing on the bone, takes up a bit of fabric. He continues to chew. Disaster! Now you've learned the lesson: dogs with chew toys have to be either kept off furniture and carpets, carefully supervised or put into their confined areas for chew time.

The wooden legs of furniture are favorite objects for chewing. The first time, tell the dog "Leave it!" (or "No!") and offer him a chew toy as a substitute. But your clever dog may be hiding under the chair and doing some silent destruction, which you may not notice until it's too late. In this case, it's time to try one of the foul-tasting products, made specifically to prevent destructive chewing, that is sprayed on the objects of your dog's chewing attention. These products also work to keep the dog away from plants, trash, etc. It's even a good way to stop the dog from "mouthing" or chewing on your hands or the leg of your pants. (Be sure to wash your hands after the mouthing lesson!) A little spray goes a long way.

Providing your Griff puppy with strong and safe chew toys prevents him from choosing "chew toys" of his own.

INDEX

*Page numbers in **boldface** indicate illustrations.*

Adenovirus 114
Adult
—adoption 84
—health 109
—training 82, 84
Advanced Agility Dog 144
Aggression 54, 84, 116, 150
Agility Dog 144
Agility Excellent 144
Agility trials 140, 142
Aging 111
Air travel 79
Albrecht of Solms-Braunfels, Prince 10
All-breed show 139
Allergies 65
Alpha role 93
American Field 15, 37
American Field Dog Stud Book 12
American Heartworm Society 131
American Kennel Club 12, 14, 30, 132, 133, 135-136, 139, 147
—breed standard 31
—Companion Animal Recovery 76
—competitive events 140
—conformation showing 134
—registration 37
American Kennel Gazette 139
American Veterinary Medical Association 52
American Wirehaired Pointing Griffon Association 12, 14, 16, 31
American-bred Class 138
Ancylostoma caninum 127, **130**
Anemia 64
Annual vet exams 109
Antifreeze 52
Appetite loss 111
Ascarid **126**, 127
Ascaris lumbricoides **126**
Attention 95, 100
Ballard, Wendy 80
Bathing 73
Beard 22
Bedding 43, 55, 90
Behavioral problems 149
Behavioral specialist 149, 152
Best in Show 134-135, 139
Best of Breed 134, 139
Bloat 66-67
Blowing coat 71
Boarding 81
Body language 84, 91, 98, 150
Body temperature 78
Bones 43
Bordetella 114
Bordetella bronchiseptica 116
Borrelia burgdorferi 114
Borreliosis 116
Bowls 41

Bred-by-Exhibitor Class 138
Breed standard 30, 32, 135
Breeder 28, 39, 135
—selection 37, 39, 107
Brushing 73
Canadian Kennel Club 14, 133
Cancer 116
Canine cough 114
Canine development schedule 85
Canine Good Citizen® Program 140
Canis domesticus 10
Canis lupus 10
Car travel 46, 77-79
Carpentier, Jacques 35
Cats 24, 29
Center for the Human-Animal Bond 22
Cesky Fousek 13-15
Champion 136, 137
Champion Tracker 145
Chesapeake Bay Retriever 16
Chew toys 43-44, 46, 60, 88, 90, 155
Chewing 43, 59, 154
Cheyletiella mite **123**
Chiggers 125
Children 22-23, 54, 56, 60, 62, 84
Class dogs 137
Classes at shows 137-138
Clipping 72
Club Français du Griffon d'Arrêt à Poil Dur Korthals 13, 35
Clubs 13-14, 135-136
Coat 21, 71
Cognitive dysfunction 111
Collar 46-47, 49, 75, 94
Color 21
Come 99, 105
Commands 95-102, 105
Commitment of ownership 39-40
Companion Dog 140-141
Competitive events 140
Conformation shows 30, 132-140
Consistency 42, 57-58, 60-61, 82, 84, 96
Core vaccines 116
Coronavirus 114, 116
Correction 93, 148
Crate 40, 41, 54-55, 62, 79, 88-89, 152
—pads 43
—training 86-93
Crying 55, 62, 89
Ctenocephalides canis **118**
Dangers in the home 50-52, 88
DEET 125
Demodex mite **125**
Demodicosis 124-125

Dental care 74, 109, 111
Destructive behavior 153
Development of breed 19
Diet 65, 67
—senior 65
Dilatation 67
Dipylidium caninum 128, **130**
Dirofilaria immitis 129, **130**, **131**
Discipline 59, 93
Distemper 114, 116
Dog clubs 136
DogGone™ newsletter 80
Dominance 36, 96, 150-151
Down 61, 90, 97-98
Down/stay 99
Dual Champion 146
Ear 22
—care of 73-74
—mites 123-124
Echinococcus multilocularis 129
Entropion 28
Estrus 116
European hunting style 17
Events Calendar 139
Excessive thirst 66
Exercise 65, 67, 69-71
—pen 88
Expenses of ownership 41
External parasites 118-125
Eye problems 28
Family meeting the puppy 53
Fear 54
—biting 150
—of water 148
—period 57
Fédération Cynologique Internationale 14-15, 31
Feeding 64-65, 67
Fenced yard 24, 52
Field Champion 146
Field Dog Stud Book 37
Field trials 140, 145
First night in new home 54
Flatbrook Kyjo's What a Sport 14
Fleas **118**, 119, **120**
Food 64-65, 67, 89
—bowls 41
—loss of interest in 111
—poisonous to dogs 51, 64
—rewards 83, 93, 97-99
Foufons 14
Foundation dogs 9-10
France 10-11, 12, 13
Free-feeding 64
French working standard 35
Gallop 22, 35
Gastric torsion 66-67
Gastropexy 67
Genetic testing 107
German Longhaired Pointer **9**
German Shorthaired Pointer **9**, 11

German Wirehaired Pointer **9**, 13, 15
Germany 10-11, 12, 13
Getting started in showing 134
Giardia 114
Gray wolf **10**
Griffon **8**
Griffon Bleu de Gascogne **9**
Griffon Club of America 13
Grooming 71
Group competition 134-135, 139
Growing pains 27
Guard dog 23
Guarding behavior 152
Gum disease 109
Gun shyness 25
Hand-stripping 72
Handler 132
Health 37, 52
—adult 109
—concerns 26-28, 67
—insurance for pets 113
—journal 53
—puppy 37, 107
—senior dog 111
Heart disease 111
Heartworm 109, 129, **130**, **131**
Heat cycle 116
Heat stroke 78
Heel 100-102
Height 20
Hepatitis 114, 116
Here command 99, 105
Heterodoxus spiniger **124**
Hip dysplasia 26-27
HomeAgain™ Companion Animal Retrieval System 76
Hookworm **127**, **130**
House-training 27, 40-41, 60, 86-93
Hunting 16-19, 27, 105
—instinct 24
—style 17
—tests 140, 147
Hunting Retriever Club 147
Identification 75-77
Indefinite Listing Privilege 29
Infectious diseases 114, 115-116
Insurance 113
Internal parasites 126-131
International Wirehaired Pointing Griffon Club 13
Irritable aggression 151
Ixodes dammini **121-122**
Jensen, Bill 17
Jerome von Herrenhausen **15**
Jogging 70
Judges 136, 138
Jumper agility titles 144
Jumping up 61, 90
Junior Hunter 147
Junior Showmanship 140
Kennel Club, The 133

Kidney problems 111
Korthals, Eduard K. 9-11, 13
Korthals Griffon 9
Korthals Patriarchs 9-10
Leash 48-49, 91, 94
—pulling on 102
Leptospirosis 114, 116
Lifespan 111
Line-breeding 10
Loneliness 153
Lost dog 75
Louse **124**
Lyme disease 114, 116
Majors 136
Mammary cancer 116
Marlow, Bill 16
Master Agility Champion 144
Master Agility Dog 144
Master Agility Excellent 144
Master Hunter 147
Microchip 76
Mindset of dogs 148
Miscellaneous Class 142
Mites **123**, 124, **125**
—infestation 74
Mosquitoes 125, 129, 131
Mounting 116
Movement 23
Multi-dog household 70
Nail clipping 74
Name 95, 101
National Obedience
 Champion 142
National Shoot to Retrieve
 Association 37
Nederlandse Griffonclub 13
Neutering 36, 109, 116-117, 140
Nipping 59, 62
Non-core vaccines 116
North American Hunting
 Retriever Association 147
North American Versatile
 Hunting Dog Association
 15, 37, 146
Novice Agility 144
Novice Class 137
Obedience 98
—classes 104
—Trial Champion 142
—trials 104, 140
Obesity 64
Off 61, 90
Okay 98, 102
Onions 64
Open Agility 144
Open Class 138
Orthopedic Foundation for
 Animals 27, 37
Other dogs 70, 116
Other pets 24, 84
Otodectes cynotis 123
Outdoor safety 52
Ovariohysterectomy 117
Ownership 39-40
—expenses of 41
—suitability 28-29
Pack animals 10, 57-59

Panosteitis 27
Paper-training 87, 91
Parainfluenza 114, 116
Parasites
—control 109
—external 117, 118-125
—internal 126-131
Parent club 14, 136, 139
Parvovirus 114, 116
Patience 82, 84
PennHIP 27, 37
Penthièvre, Duke of 10
Personality 22-24
Pet dogs 18
Physical traits 20-22
Plants 49, 51
Playtime 99
Poisons 49, 50-52, 64
Positive reinforcement 54, 93,
 95, 149
Possessive behavior 152
Practicing 99
—commands 96
Praise 82-83, 93, 148-149
Preventive care 107, 109, 111
Prey drive 24, 29
Problem behavior 149
Proglottid **129**
Prostate problems 116
Pudelpointer **9**
Pulling on leash 102
Punishment 63, 93-94, 152
Puppy 59-63
—common problems 59
—establishing leadership 57-
 59, 82
—field potential 37
—first car ride 46
—first night in new home 54
—health 37, 107
—meeting the family 53
—personality 39, 109
—selection 36-39, 107
—show quality 132-133, 137
—socialization 56
—supplies for 40
—teething 60
—temperament 38
—training 54, 58, 82, 95
Puppy Class 137
Puppy-proofing 27, 49
Pure-bred dog 32
Quartering 35
Rabies 52, 114, 116
Rawhide 44
Registration 37
Requirements for show 139
Rescue 7
Reserve Winners Bitch 138
Reserve Winners Dog 138
Retriever field trials 146
Retrieving 70
Rewards 82-83
—food 93, 97-99
Rhabditis **130**
Roading 35
Roaming 116

Robotic dog 22
Roca, Phillipe 12
Rogers, Thomas 13
Rope toys 44
Roundworm **126**, 127, **130**
Routine 42, 60, 84
Royal Belgium Griffon Club 13
Running style 35
Russian Setter (Griffon) 12
Safety 49, 64, 78, 88, 90, 99,
 155
—at home 50-52
—in hot weather 78
—in the car 79
—outdoors 24, 52
—with toys 43, 44
Sarcoptes scabiei **123**
Scabies 123
Scent attraction 91
Schedule 42, 60, 84, 86
Senior dog
—diet 65
—healthcare 111
Senior Hunter 147
Separation anxiety 152-154
Sex-related differences 20, 25,
 36, 37
Shedding 71-72
Show quality 132-133, 137
Shows, conformation 132-134
—classes at 137-138, 139
Sit 95
Sit/stay 98
Size 20
Skin allergies 65
Socialization 27, 54, 56, 58, 95,
 109, 150
Soft toys 44
Spaying 109, 116-117, 140
Specials 139
Specialty show 136
Spinone Italiano **11**
Split among breed fanciers
 11, 13
Standard 32, 135
Stay 98, 102
Stomach stapling 67
Stray dog 75
Stripping 72
Supervision 60, 90
Surgery 117
Swimming 69, 148
Taenia pisiformis **129**
Tail 21
Tapeworm 128, **129**, **130**
Tattoo 77
Teeth 74, 109, 111
Teething period 60, 155
Temperament 22-24, 38, 149
—evaluation 109
Temperature 78
Territorial aggression 151
Testicular cancer 116
Thirst 66
Tick-borne diseases 121
Ticks **121-122**
Timing 82, 91, 100, 148

Toxascaris leonine 126
Toxins 49, 50-52, 64
Toxocara canis **126**
Toys 43-44, 46, 60, 88, 90, 155
Tracking 140, 145
Tracking Dog 145
Tracking Dog Excellent 145
Training 24, 58, 60
—basic principles of 82
—commands 95-102, 105
—consistency in 57, 61, 96
—crate 40, 89
—early 58
—for the field 105
—importance of timing 91, 100, 148
—potty 27, 86-93
—proper attitude 95
—puppy 54, 82, 92
Traveling 42, 46, 76, 77-81
Treats 54, 65, 82-83, 93
Trichuris sp. **128**
Type 132-133
Types of shows 136
United Kennel Club 14, 37, 133, 147
—Pointing Dog Program 144
United States 12-16
United States Dog Agility
 Association 142
University of Pennsylvania's Hip
 Improvement Program 27, 37
Urine marking 116
Utility Dog 141
Utility Dog Excellent 142
Vacations 76, 80
Vaccinations 52-53, 57, 109, 114,
 115-116
Versatile Hunting Dog 146
Versatile Surface Tracking 145
Veterinarian 44, 46, 52, 109-113,
 115, 149
Veterinary insurance 113
Visiting the litter 39
Voice 95
Volvulus 67
Walker, Mrs. Helen Whitehouse
 140
Water 22, 66-67, 89, 148
—bowls 41
—increased intake 66
Weather-related problems 78
West Nile virus 114
Westminster Kennel Club 12, 134
Whoa command 105
Whining 55, 62, 89
Whipworm **128**
Winners Bitch 138
Winners Class 138
Winners Dog 138
Wirehaired Pointing Griffon 8
—Fousek cross 15
Wirehaired Pointing Griffon Club
 of America 13, 14-15
Wolf 10
Working standard 35
World Wars 11, 12, 13, 14
Worm control 128
Zoletta 12, 19

My Wirehaired Pointing Griffon

PUT YOUR PUPPY'S FIRST PICTURE HERE

Dog's Name _____

Date _____ Photographer _____